PARENT *with* CONFIDENCE

POWER TOOLS FOR BRINGING UP GREAT KIDS

CAROLYN BOND

Parent with Confidence: *Power Tools for Bringing Up Great Kids*

Website for book: *www.parentwithconfidence.com* and *www.howtobringupgreatkids.com*

Published by Norris Publishing

ISBN 978-0-9947467-0-2

Copy Editing: M.K.Hughes
Developmental Editing: HPGrauel
Front Cover Photograph: Shutterstock/mihalec
Cover Design and Interior Layout: AuthorSupport.com

TABLE OF CONTENTS

PART THREE Next Steps

INTRODUCTION

Do you often find yourself yelling at your kids? Giving orders? Making demands?

Do they frustrate you by refusing to cooperate?

Do you feel guilty because of something you wish you'd handled differently?

Do you wish that you had a happier child or happier family life?

You're not alone.

There are tons of parents out there who have feelings just like yours. I remember the same frustrations, discouragement, and guilt that you may feel. I also remember the relief I experienced when I discovered a way to parent more effectively. Although I had degrees in sociology and social work and had all the best intentions, the way in which I handled my children wasn't working. The boys fought constantly and there were food and bedtime problems, too. No amount of cajoling, bribing, or punishing would help. I became a yeller, and a hand and bottom slapper. I felt helpless.

Parenting is not taught in school, yet it's the most important life work we have. We either parent the way we were raised or we resolve to do it differently. No wonder we struggle! Often, we're just at our wits' end, caught in our moments, wondering what to do. We need realistic solutions to help us raise our kids—and to start enjoying parenting, because it can be joyful!

I was extremely fortunate to have the chance to join a parenting course by two parenting experts—a medical doctor and a psychologist. The course was based on the approach of Alfred Adler and Rudolf Dreikurs, whose parenting and family principles have been studied and followed all over the world for more than fifty years. Adler, and his student Dreikurs, considered parents and children to be equals and believed that children's behavior is directly related to their feelings of belonging in the family—if children feel valued and respected, their behavior improves. Democratic parenting produces children with high self-esteem, respect for themselves and others, and problem-solving skills that will serve them into adulthood. After I implemented this parenting philosophy in my own home, the positive results I saw led me to more than twenty years of further study, and to helping hundreds of parents with the principles outlined in this book.

This book is full of easily accessible parenting tools, with examples that illustrate problems and solutions—so you'll see them in action and can implement the techniques yourself.

Clear and direct suggestions are provided to help you start to make positive changes in your family. My four great kids are a testament to the power of this approach.

The first step is to read and understand Part One where I've outlined the basics of the democratic system to raising your children. Then, in Part Two, you'll delve into the practical work with the steps I've outlined—steps that lead to more effective parenting and a joyous, harmonious family.

PART ONE

A Need to Belong: Setting the Stage to Grow Great Kids

CHAPTER ONE

The Power of Treating Your Child as an Equal

You're bigger, older, and more competent than your child. You may have traveled, graduated from high school or university, or have tradesmen's papers. You may be an electrician, a doctor, office worker, a banker, teacher, or a construction worker.

Your child, on the other hand, is small. He may be a newborn baby or a preteen. He has a lot to learn in so many ways. He may not even be able to walk or talk yet.

Here is the crunch: **you and your child are equals**. You're both human beings, although one of you has had more experience than the other. Just because she exists, your daughter deserves the same respect you do and the opportunity to make choices for herself. She is no less important than you. **You are not superior**. This is a basic premise that is difficult for many people to really understand. But when you start to think about it, it makes perfect sense.

What does being an equal mean? Letting kids make choices at a young age? Does this democratic approach to parenting mean that children can do whatever they want? Is it the same as permissiveness? Absolutely not! Permissive parents are those who can't enforce boundaries. Because they're unable to establish consistent limits, their households are run in a haphazard, inconsistent manner. Respectful parents create realistic and healthy boundaries, allowing their children freedom within those limits.

Let's look at democracy as it pertains to government. If we live in a democracy, we have freedom to choose who governs us, our jobs, the route to work, what we eat, when we eat and work, what car to drive, and so on. But we live with certain laws that are put in place to produce order and encourage respect for each other, such as traffic laws, requirements for food production and handling, and all the other structures that make it easier and safer to live together on the same planet. If we were each allowed to do everything we wanted, we would live in chaos.

In a democratic family, we also have structure and rules for living together. We have mealtimes, bedtimes, and quiet times for sleep and so on. We are able to make these rules as a family and teach our children to live within this framework so we have basic order and routine in our family life.

If we respect our children as our equals in terms of deserving dignity and respect, we learn to allow our children to make great choices within the framework of family order. They'll respond so positively that you'll be amazed at how family life will flourish!

> *Three-year-old Nadia didn't want to put on her snowsuit. Her mother, Jess, had a doctor's appointment and they had to go out into the snowy morning. Before changing her parenting methods, Jess would have wrestled Nadia onto her knee and into the snowsuit. Nadia would have then resisted even more, and both would have ended up exhausted and unhappy. Instead, Jess offered her a choice. "Which leg goes in first, Nadia? This one or that one?" Nadia became interested in the choice and pointed to her left leg. She happily put her leg in and soon was dressed to go out.*

You might say that Jess manipulated Nadia into doing what she wanted her to do, but Jess's handling of the situation roots itself in respect, order, and democracy. She didn't ask Nadia if she'd like to get into her snowsuit. That was not an option. She offered her a choice within the limits of safety and avoided having to use her power and her size to make Nadia behave. Instead, Nadia felt she had input in making the decision about dressing for the cold. Jess empowered Nadia!

> *In potty training her two-year-old Jason, Helen was under pressure. Daycare enrollment was fast approaching and the rule for registering the child was that he be diaper-*

free. She felt stressed and fearful about introducing him to the potty because she had read it was very difficult and had heard some negative feedback from friends about their experiences. Her insecurity was communicated to Jason and, when he resisted sitting on the potty, she tried to use power to make him sit. Jason screamed and refused to cooperate.

If Jason doesn't want to potty train, there is absolutely no way to make him do it. It really is his business and **he needs to be inspired to learn to use the toilet.** What could Helen do to introduce Jason to the toilet? If she and her husband are comfortable with their bodies and want to teach Jason that bodily functions are natural, she could show him how she uses the toilet and also how his daddy goes to the toilet. She can introduce him to the potty and ask him if he would like to try it, or if he would like to sit on the big toilet or stand on the step-stool and go like Daddy. She can ask him if he'd like to wear big-boy pants like Daddy or go without a diaper and be pants-free for the rest of the day.

Her attitude is very important, and she'll gain great results if she is natural and easygoing. If Jason isn't interested at all, she puts potty training aside for a few days or a week and then repeats the process. Eventually, Jason's interest is piqued and he chooses his preferred way of starting to toilet train. She keeps quiet between times and doesn't nag or scold him for his lack of interest when changing his diaper. Soon, Jason asks to use the potty chair.

In this example, **Jason's mother respects him** and his readiness for toilet training. She uses humor and love while encouraging her son. She has put a lot of thought into it beforehand, and realizes that she must be low key, friendly, and consistent in reminding herself that toilet training is Jason's business. And, if he's not interested, if he isn't given ownership over this decision, no amount of effort on Helen's part will make it happen.

You may resist the idea of using the toilet in front of your child or having him go naked for a day or two. If so, you can offer him the choice between the big toilet and the potty, and you might have a story he can choose to have you read while he sits. Again, if he resists, don't push. Just calmly continue to change his diaper without making any comments about toilet training.

You may wonder if you could ever be that relaxed about training. As we progress through other examples, you'll catch on and will gradually start to think in a new way.

REMINDERS:

✓ **Giving children orders and being pushy simply doesn't work**
✓ **If children feel valued and respected as a vital part of the family, they will want to learn and cooperate**

You can help your children feel like valued members of the family by refusing to punish and criticize, and by learning how to be more encouraging. I'll show you how in the next chapter.

CHAPTER TWO

The Power of Recognition

One of the key fundamentals in effective child rearing is **recognizing how vital it is for your child to feel that he is valued as part of your family group.** He wants to feel that he is important and respected in his role in the family, even though he may be very young.

> *If Sara feels a part of the family, she doesn't need to act out to get attention. She is noticed and appreciated just because she exists. Both parents are aware of her need for love and appreciation and make sure that, every day, she knows how much she is cherished.*

What happens if Sara feels that her new baby brother is preferred? What happens when her mother is breastfeeding or rocking the baby? As the first child, Sara is used to having her parents' attention all to herself. She now has to share it. She needs her parents' help.

Sara's parents can take turns giving her extra time. They can show her they value her as their "big girl" and show her how many things she can do that the baby can't. Perhaps she can be taken on an outing without the baby. Perhaps she can help Mommy with the new baby's care in some way or help with the preparation of a meal. Her parents are sensitive to her feelings of insecurity and make sure she doesn't feel set aside by the arrival of her brother.

If Sara's needs aren't met, she may try some ways to get her parents' attention. Without being consciously aware of what she's doing, she may act like a baby or begin to misbehave. **If her parents react and give her attention for the misbehavior, she misbehaves again because she was successful in getting them to notice her.** This is the seed of Sara's future relationship with her parents unless they understand and help her with her feeling of abandonment.

One of the best ways you can help your child feel worthy is to spend time with him. You can cook together or bake cookies, for example, or even do a household chore. You're having fun, he is learning a skill, and you are letting him know how much you enjoy his company.

Listening with your full attention is another skill to practice. If you're in conversation with a friend who keeps looking at his watch, getting calls on his phone, and looking everywhere but at you, you know how devalued you feel. Your child needs you to look him in the eyes and give him your full attention in the moment that he is talking with you. Shut your phone off if you have to and go to a quiet place so you can focus on what he is communicating.

> *Ryan and Natalie were very excited. Their dad was taking them to a movie! They flew into their coats and hats and arrived about twenty minutes early at the theater. Dad bought them each a treat and they settled into their seats. Dad had brought the Saturday newspaper with him and took it out to read while they waited. The children vainly attempted to talk with him but soon gave up. His cell phone rang and he spent the rest of their waiting time talking on his phone.*

What impression do children receive when treated this way by their parents? They feel they're not important enough to talk with and they feel left out. Does this father behave in such a manner when out with his friends? I doubt it. He didn't seem to know that he was falling down on the job.

When you're with your children, be *with* them. Kids can be wonderfully entertaining and enjoyable.

> *Jim had had an exhausting day at the office. He was late arriving home because traffic was heavy and someone had cut him off. He was still angry when he pulled into his driveway. He opened the door to find his two sons waiting for him. Knowing how much they wanted to play, and feeling extremely tired, he knelt down, hugged them, and said, "I've had a bad day, guys, and I'm very tired. I know you want to play but I need to go and have a rest right*

now. In a while, when I get up, we'll have some time to play before dinner. Let's set the timer. When the bell rings, come and get me and we'll play." The timer was set and the boys quietly amused themselves with their toys while they waited for the timer to ring.

Jim knew he couldn't give his sons his full attention when he was feeling so tired. Instead, **treating them with great respect, he explained his situation and offered an alternative** that would make all of them happy.

Coming in the door after school on a wintry day, ten-year-old Belinda and eight-year-old Simon were looking forward to telling their mother about their day. They had hardly closed the door when they heard her call, "Hang up your coats and put your boots away!"

The above example is repeated thousands of times every wintry or rainy day. I wonder, would mother would greet her neighbor that way when she came to the door? **If you take a moment to think before speaking and think how you would like to be spoken to,** you might consider treating your children the same way you would treat a friend. Treat your children in the way you, yourself, would like to be treated. If you have an atmosphere of cooperation in your home, you won't have to nag or remind your children.

REMINDERS:

✓ Ensure that your child feels valued and important in his or her role in the family

✓ Give attention for positive behavior, not for misbehavior

✓ Spend time with your child, giving your full attention

✓ Explain your position, don't give orders that aren't understood

✓ Speak to your child with courtesy as you or your friends would like to be spoken to

CHAPTER THREE

The Power of Appreciation

It feels wonderful to be on the receiving end of encouragement. We all respond positively, basking in the glow of having been noticed and appreciated. When it comes to **giving** encouragement, however, we sometimes miss the opportunity, perhaps because we're in the habit of commenting on negatives instead of positives.

Encouragement is a skill that we can all learn more about. To most of us it just doesn't come naturally. We may have been raised in a family that noticed mistakes and used criticism as a way of "motivating" better behavior. If we don't know another way, we usually do the same with our own children.

Hold your criticism. No one likes being criticized. Think about how you feel at work or in a social setting when you're on the receiving end of criticism, then transfer that knowledge to better understand your kids. "Constructive" criticism is also discouraging, as you likely know from experience; whatever is missing or not completely correct is noticed and those "helpful" suggestions can make a person feel small.

How do we help children to learn if we don't criticize? **Completely cease pointing out anything negative.** To balance the scales, **notice any behavior that you approve of or that is a positive action on the part of your child.** Interestingly enough, she will respond with more good behavior and positive results as she finds she gets noticed and feels she is appreciated by the family. **When bad behavior is not rewarded, it dies from lack of feeding.**

Don't punish. Many psychologists agree that a child who misbehaves is unhappy and discouraged rather than "bad." He feels left out, slighted, and often unwanted. Poor behavior is a child's call for help, not just something to irritate a parent. His misbehavior gets him more attention than his good behavior. **Punishing doesn't work as it only discourages him further.** A snowball effect results until parent and child are in a futile and frustrating power struggle.

When you punish, you're not treating your child as an equal. You're bigger and more powerful, and are using your size and power to make him do what you want. Put yourself in his place. How do you feel if someone gives you orders or takes away a privilege? Certainly there are more productive and tactful ways to cultivate cooperation. Your child will want to help, to have good manners, and to be kind to his brother, for example, if his positive actions are noticed and encouraged.

We often treat our children in a negative way. Sometimes we resort to humiliation and put-downs, which are a form of punishment too. This only makes the situation worse. If we become conscious of our attitude and what we're saying, we find that countless times each day we may point out to our children what they're doing wrong. We rarely recognize what they're doing right. This only makes the situation worse.

Misbehavior is usually a subconscious reaction to a feeling of being left out or not valued. It can give a pay-off in being noticed, even if it means being punished. You can turn this situation around simply by assessing the needs of your child and making a few changes in your attitudes and behaviors. **Pay attention to positives and they grow while the negatives shrink.**

How do you encourage your child? The basis of encouraging your child is recognizing something positive that he has done. Even if he is the "bad one," he has something that he does that you can recognize and appreciate. **You stop noticing his misbehavior.** You make sure that you tell him about anything that he does that you appreciate, even if it's the way he combs his hair. Catch your critical remark before it escapes and find something favorable to take its place.

The key is to hold your tongue when you don't approve and to speak out when there's something that your child does that you like. Do I mean that you ignore negative behavior? Yes! This could be a shocking suggestion for some parents. It's an entirely new idea to many people. But it is an idea that has great value and helps prevent discouragement in your child.

The kids were playing with their blocks and Legos and it was very quiet as Renata looked in the family room door. In the old days, she wouldn't have entered the room unless someone shouted or there was an argument. She might have tiptoed past the door for fear of disturbing the peaceful scene. Instead, she entered the room and said, "What fun you're having!" patting them on the head and giving each of them a little hug. The children hugged her back and showed her the large tower they were making. After admiring their work, she then went on her way, leaving a happy feeling in the family room. She found that by noticing good behavior, the incidents of fighting and arguing lessened significantly.

Children, like all of us, want to belong and want to contribute and help. It's only when their efforts in this direction are not recognized that they seek attention through negative behavior. It may not be the kind of attention they want, but it's better than no attention at all!

To help you to begin to be more encouraging, try out the following method. For one week, choose one person in your family and consciously encourage him or her. It could be a child or even your spouse or partner. Point out whenever possible how he is being helpful, happy, responsible, constructive, imaginative, or cooperative. Avoid criticism at all costs. You'll love the results!

There's a difference between encouragement and praise that makes encouragement more helpful to your child. See the difference in the following two examples:

A. Melody brought home her colorful painting from school and showed it to her parents. "You're such a good artist!" gushed her mother. "You must be the best artist in the whole class!" said Daddy. Melody knew that she wasn't a great artist. Her friend's picture was much better than hers. Her parents' reaction seemed false, somehow.

B. Melody brought home her colorful painting from school and showed it to her parents. "I love the colors, honey," said her mother. "It looks as if you really enjoyed painting this!" said Dad. Melody happily helped them put her artwork on the fridge.

In the above examples, you can see Melody's parents use praise in the first and encouragement in the second. Although this difference may seem to be difficult to understand, you can catch on with a little practice. **Encouragement notices the** *action.* **Praise focuses on the** *actor.* In other words, encourage the things your child does. Avoid focusing on the child herself. Avoid "Good girl!" Say, "Thanks for your help," "I like your story," or "I really enjoy being with you." Do you see the difference? Children who hear "good girl" or "good boy" all the time end up asking, "Am I a good girl?" or "Am I a good boy?" and require the praise. If they don't hear it they become discouraged and feel they don't measure up in some way. They may then choose misbehavior to get attention. It's subtle but you'll catch on before long. Just start to listen to yourself. **Make a small beginning and build on it one step at a time. Your child will have elevated self-esteem and a strong sense of being valued.** He won't have to misbehave to get your attention.

REMINDERS:

- ✓ Learn to give encouragement by recognizing positives
- ✓ Hold your criticism
- ✓ Don't punish. It doesn't work
- ✓ Children want to contribute and help. Notice their efforts
- ✓ Learn to encourage rather than praise
- ✓ To help you learn how to encourage, choose a person in your family and recognize all positive things he or she does for an entire week

CHAPTER FOUR

The Power of Training

If we're not criticizing and we're not punishing, how do we help our children to learn the things they need to know to become valuable, respectful, contributing members of society?

First, consciously become a role model for your children in your words and behavior. If you don't want them to swear, avoid swearing in front of them. Don't kick the dog or throw something when you're angry. It's better to do nothing than the wrong thing. The old advice to count to ten before reacting is helpful because it gives you time to think.

Demonstrate your affection for your spouse and children. Be free with hugs, kisses, and compliments. If you're in a situation of marriage breakdown, refrain from arguing in front of the children. Don't treat your children as confidants or "best friends." Always be respectful to your spouse when he or she is present and in the way you talk when he or she isn't there.

Your child is extremely observant. If you shake the hand of someone you meet, likely she'll offer a hand as well. Your demonstration of manners is noticed and imitated by her.

"Andrew, sit up straight. Stop slouching! Put your napkin on your lap," admonished Jim, as the family sat down to Thanksgiving dinner at his parents' home. A little later, seeing Andrew wiping his greasy hands on his mother's best tablecloth made Jim livid. He realized that his boys had no idea how to sit properly at the table and use cutlery effectively. Throughout dinner, he nagged them incessantly, feeling embarrassed and guilty at their lack of training. The whole family was on edge and the atmosphere grew tenser as the meal progressed.

At a time that isn't associated with a meal, you need to teach your kids table manners. You can teach them, in an atmosphere of friendliness and love, how to remove hats before sitting down, how to use a table napkin properly, how to hold a knife and fork, how to chew with mouths closed, and all of the other things that are necessary to know when eating at a table with others. **Always teach manners at home and not in front of guests or out in public.** When they're young, kids love a tea party which is a great place for learning. Remember to think how you would feel in a situation if you were corrected or reprimanded in front of others. If your child forgets his manners in public, ignore it. Your reputation doesn't depend on your child's table manners. Remember to **notice the positive things** your child did or said when you get home to encourage his efforts in the right direction.

Nancy found herself reminding Jacob, eleven, on a daily basis to remember his homework when he left for school in the morning. If he forgot it she usually got dressed and drove to his school where she left it for him to pick up in the school office. One day she decided to put into practice a new idea she had learned at the parenting group. She knew that she needed to help Jacob learn to be more responsible. She said, "Jacob, I think you're old enough to remember to take your homework to school. If you think that you can learn to remember it yourself, I won't nag you about it anymore." Jacob thought about it and agreed that it really was his business, not his mom's. "Okay, Jacob. I'm backing off and won't mention it again," said Nancy. When Jacob forgot his homework again the next day, she agonized about his not remembering it but stuck to her guns and didn't deliver it to him. When Jacob arrived home after school, Nancy held herself back and didn't mention the forgotten homework. Jacob said, "Mom, I forgot my homework again. The teacher made me stay in at lunchtime and I didn't get to go to chess club!" The next day, Jacob remembered to put his homework in his backpack. Nancy made sure that she recognized the step forward, saying, "Hurray! You remembered! Good for you!"

What's your reaction to the above story? Was Nancy unkind in letting Jacob go without his homework and not reminding him? Do you think an eleven year old should be reminded every day to remember the things he needs? Nancy courageously decided to train her son and did so while remaining friendly and not mentioning his oversight. Jacob experienced the natural negative consequence imparted by his teacher, which is a better motivator than his mother's nagging.

Vera always called John, fifteen, in the morning to get him up for school. She went down to his room on the lower level of the house, knocked on the door, and told him it was time to wake up. He was always grumpy and bad tempered, which started Vera's day on a bad footing. One day, she read an article about training children to be responsible for their own schedules. She realized that she was doing John a disservice by doing something for him that he could do himself. She needed to encourage his independence. She and John discussed the article and John decided that he could get himself up from that point on. Vera told him that she knew he could do it. She made sure he knew how to set his alarm and waited in the kitchen for him to appear the next morning. She was thrilled to see John's smile and his pride in getting up and getting ready for school on his own and made sure to let him know how pleased she was.

There are so many examples of parents doing for children the things that they could do for themselves. Children are intelligent, resourceful beings. They can do much more than we give them credit for in daily life. As an experiment, ask your preteen to do the grocery shopping for you. You could sit down and make the grocery list together if she'd like to and discuss the various items needed. She'll likely do a wonderful job, even comparing prices, if she's gone shopping with you in the past.

It's important to give your child time to "be." I recently heard about a current parenting method that encourages parents to hold their babies constantly for the first six months. A young mother I know, Becky, had embraced this idea and carried her daughter all day, even holding her while she napped. When her friends would call her to invite her to go shopping or to a movie, Becky was unavailable. She'd decided to put her own life on hold so she could be at home to carry her baby and told her friends she had no time to go out with them. Unfortunately, Becky was teaching her child to be wholly reliant on her. **Children deserve to be trained to spend time alone if they're going to be self-reliant adults.**

> *Sylvia was at her limit at a parent study group meeting. "I have no time to myself!" she cried. She was amusing and playing with her twenty-four-month-old daughter, Anastasia, all day long and complained of no time to clean the house or cook dinner. She had resorted to cooking the meals for the following day after she put Anastasia to bed, spending all evening in the kitchen. She felt pressured and tired out, asking for ideas to change her situation.*

Even very young babies need to learn to have their own space. To help them learn to enjoy their own company, a playpen is invaluable. You can place your baby in a playpen with mobiles and toys for short times as part of the daily routine from the time she's just a few weeks old. Babies learn to enjoy their time alone out of harm's way and parents can have time to themselves as well, either to relax or get some work done.

Passing by the playpen from time to time with a smile and a cheerful word helps encourage this independence.

You'll discover that training your kids can be fun. When my second son was about seven, we did a lot of baking together. We loved spending the time together; he ended up being able to bake cakes without my supervision. We had lots of great desserts and it was the beginning of his love of cooking, I'm sure!

Training children takes time, I know, but it's so worth it. You'll raise children who have good manners, respect others, and are capable of tasks beyond anything you could imagine.

REMINDERS:

- ✓ Be a good role model. Your children are watching you!
- ✓ To teach your kids about love, be affectionate with your partner or spouse in front of them
- ✓ Have learning sessions at home to teach manners. Make it fun!
- ✓ Train kids to observe routine. Show them how to use alarm clocks and timers to help them gain independence
- ✓ Don't overprotect. Even young babies can be trained to enjoy time alone
- ✓ Recognize the positive. Ignore the negative

CHAPTER FIVE

The Power of Inspiration

Have you got a grumpy child? Parents who frequently give their kids orders often find that they're met with frowns, sulking, and disobedience. Going back to the basic idea of respecting your child and treating him as an equal, we find something fundamental you can do to generate cooperation and learning: **stop giving orders. Instead, decide what *your* action will be, tell the children once, and then take action.**

Georgia had been practicing a new way to handle the noisy behavior in the car. Before, when she had been driving her two boys Johnny, eight, and Nate, six, to activities, she took her attention off the road to give pointless orders to stop their rambunctious behavior. Now once again on the way to swimming lessons, the noise level in the car was rising. She put on the blinkers, pulled over to the side of the road, and stopped the car. "Why are we stopping, Mommy?" asked Nate. "I will not drive the car when boys are noisy," said Georgia. "We'll be late, Mom!" said Johnny in a worried voice. "We'll be quiet, Mommy," said Nate. When the boys sat quietly for a minute, Georgia started the car and drove on. From that time on, all Georgia had to do was stop the car when the boys were too noisy. Instead of yelling at them, she made a decision as to what **she** *would do. Soon the car rides to lessons were more pleasant. Georgia had stopped giving her attention to misbehavior. She stopped trying to control the situation by giving orders that were ignored.*

I remember a time as a single mom when I was having trouble with my three children misbehaving at the dinner table. They were noisy, with the eldest baiting the middle one who reacted by yelling, with my youngest telling them both to be quiet. I had learned a way to handle it, and was ready to try it. I stood up saying, "I don't stay at the table with kids who act like that." I then took my plate, went into the bathroom, and shut the door. Immediately, they came to the bathroom door and said, "Come out, Mommy! We'll be good!" I waited a few minutes then, when all was quiet, I went back to the table. After that when hijinks started at the table, all I had to do was rise from my chair. The kids immediately quietened down and all was peaceful.

Why not do what works instead of constantly yelling? **Yelling doesn't work. It gives kids attention for misbehavior.** When you change your thinking and begin to **state what you will do**, the balance shifts. You've taken control and removed the attention the kids get from negative behavior. What's important is that you don't talk about it at all. You simply act. **But do remember the crucial part of recognizing good or acceptable behavior.** Children want to feel a sense of belonging. They want to feel valued and recognized as important parts of the family group. Anything that they do to contribute to a happy family life needs to be mentioned. "Thank you for keeping me company," "I enjoy being with you," "We had fun tonight, didn't we?" are all examples of phrases that will encourage your child. Why would he want to misbehave to get your attention if you are giving it out positively and consistently? He simply doesn't need to.

When babies begin to walk, a whole new world opens up to them and they start to explore their environments. We all know to remove ornaments and anything portable that is off limits when this stage arrives. How do we train babies to leave the TV alone or not to play in the potted plants? When parents start giving orders to babies, they soon find that raising their voices may work the first time, but the novelty of touching and tasting exciting new things makes babies go back to the forbidden objects anyway. Slapping their hands and saying, "Bad boy!" or "Bad girl!" as many people do, also doesn't work for the long term. That style of parenting begins a habit of punishing that can escalate over time. So, what will work?

Remember that you are **training** your young child. Instead of sitting in your armchair and calling across the room to tell him to stop, you have to **move and remove!** In other words, you get up, go to him, pick him up, and remove him from the tempting area.

Angela's fifteen-month-old daughter Robin had recently graduated from cruising around the furniture to walking on her own. All of a sudden Angela's life had changed dramatically. She needed to "baby proof" her home and train Robin not to touch things that might hurt her or that she could harm. When Robin touched the TV controls, Angela said calmly, "No, Robin," got up from her chair, and lifted her away. Robin continued to go back to the TV, looking at her mother as if this were a game. Angela said, "No, Robin. Don't touch." She then carried her and placed her in the playpen. The next time that Robin touched the TV, Angela immediately put her in the playpen. It wasn't long before Robin decided to stay away from the television. Angela had trained her by taking action without anger or raising her voice.

Taking action, moving into the situation, and removing a child who endangers herself is a normal reflex action for parents. Transfer that to any situation where you need to train your child to stay away from something she could damage.

Often children will touch forbidden things as a means to get attention. If you've been on the telephone for a while, or have had guests, for example, and haven't had time to spend with your little one, she may do things that she shouldn't do just to get you to notice her. In that case, **don't react, remain calm, and remove her from the situation. Remember to give her attention when she's cooperating.** Even if you're very busy, ten minutes now and then throughout the day spent reading a story or playing with a toy will give her some needed time with you.

If you're involved in a project and something doesn't work, you'll choose another route. This same idea will inspire cooperation and responsibility in your child. When young children are learning, there's no better training than failure. **Unless there are dangerous consequences to a child's decision, it's a good idea to stand back and let him learn for himself.** Rudolf Dreikurs, in his book *Children: The Challenge*, calls this letting "natural consequences" lead to learning. He suggests that you step back and ask yourself what would happen if you didn't interfere.

For example, if your child dawdles and is late for school, the natural consequence is that the school will use some method to ensure that lateness doesn't become a habit—for example, keeping him in at recess or lunch hour. It's his business to get to school on time and he'll soon learn to watch the clock. If he chooses not to wear gloves on a cold morning, the natural result is cold hands. You don't comment or intervene. No more nagging and reminding. It won't be necessary.

If there's danger involved and he could be hurt, you may need to step in and arrange a consequence for his misbehavior. This is what Dreikurs calls a "logical consequence."

Jeremy, nine, loved his new bike. He and his family lived in a house on a corner lot. He was allowed to ride his bike on the quiet streets away from the main road that passed in front of his home but had promised his parents he wouldn't ride on the busy main street. One day, seeing some bigger kids ride by on the main street, he decided to disobey the rule and venture out there on his bike. His dad was shocked to see him in busy traffic and called him into the house. "Jeremy, we agreed that you could ride your bike on the quiet streets but not on the main road. You chose to break our agreement so your bike will stay in the garage." After a week without the bike, Jeremy promised he'd stay off the busy thoroughfare. His father returned the bike.

Obviously, Jeremy's dad couldn't let a natural consequence take place so he had to think of a way that would inspire cooperation. The logical result of breaking the rule was that Jeremy lost his privilege to ride the bike. When he had some time to think about it and suffer the consequences of his decision to break the rule, his parents allowed him to have the bike again.

Logical consequences MUST be related to the misbehavior. If kids don't brush their teeth, you don't restrict their TV time. TV and teeth brushing have nothing to do with each other. This turns a learning experience into punishment. What could be related to tooth brushing that would produce a willingness to brush? A natural consequence wouldn't work here because lack of brushing leads to cavities. What would be a good solution? Treats could be restricted for kids who don't brush. This logical solution needs to be discussed in a friendly, conciliatory tone. "You've decided not to clean your teeth. Kids who don't brush don't get candy or cookies."

If kids' bedroom floors aren't free of clothes and their stuff, and the policy of the household is that floors are picked up the day before vacuuming, the floor doesn't get vacuumed because it's impossible to do so. You tell them that you can't find your way through to get their dirty clothes so their laundry isn't done. If this goes on more than once or twice, you may decide to pick their things up yourself, because regular cleaning is necessary for health.

You don't know where to put them though, and don't have time to figure it out, so you put anything that's on the floor into a bag and put the bag away in the storage closet or basement. You could say in a neutral tone, "Since you've decided not to pick up your room, your stuff is in the bag." Kids don't like to feel their way into a bag to get their things. This would be classified as punishment if it's voiced in an angry, punishing tone. In this case, **the kids are suffering the results of their own decision** not to pick up their stuff. The object is not to punish, but to motivate proper behavior. You're training and stimulating cooperation.

Anytime you use an "I told you so!" voice, you're punishing your child, not training her. Be very, very careful when you use logical consequences. If you have a relationship with your child that isn't favorable right now, wait until things improve before you even consider it. Develop friendlier relations first before tackling issues like messy bedrooms. Ignore the bedroom until the time is right. Notice anything at all that she does that's positive and show your appreciation.

Don't try everything at once! Start with one thing at a time. Encouraging a child comes first and continues forever. Only when you have a friendlier relationship should you even think of using logical consequences or it will seem like punishment to your discouraged child. Just turn a blind eye to some things right now. In good time, if you've stopped punishing and criticizing and started to notice and remark on anything your child does that's positive, all kinds of good things will start to happen. When a child feels valued, his behavior changes for the better because he's getting attention for behaving, not misbehaving.

REMINDERS:

- ✓ Stop giving orders. Decide what *you* will do and act
- ✓ Yelling at the kids is giving attention for misbehavior. Don't do it
- ✓ If it's safe, stand back and let kids suffer the consequences of their decisions
- ✓ If it isn't safe, think of a logical consequence related to the misdeed. Use a calm, neutral tone
- ✓ Remember to encourage the kids—*constantly!*
- ✓ Give attention for positive actions. Ignore the negatives

PART TWO

Putting It Into Action:
Handling Common Problems

CHAPTER SIX

How to Stop Fighting

Consider this moment from my previous life:

Ah-h-h. Finally. I've got some time to weed the garden. Also, I've got three flats of blooms waiting to be planted. I love gardening so much! The colors of the flowers, the smell of the soil—I inhale the whole experience.

The boys are settled in front of the TV and are quiet for now. Oh no! There it is again! That scream can bring me from any part of the house or yard. Once more I'm interrupted in my work in the garden. Will I ever be able to have some time to myself? Okay, here I come!!

They're in the TV room. Neddie, four, is crying. "Jason hit me, Mommy!" His crying is getting louder. Poor little man—always being picked on by his older brother. I hug him and give Jason the evil eye. "Jason, stop picking on your brother! Leave him alone or I'll send you to your room!" Neddie snuggles into my neck and stops his crying. "I didn't do anything, Mommy! He started it," says Jason, tears forming in his eyes. This happens too often and I don't believe him. He is six and should know better. I put Neddie down, order Jason to leave Neddie alone, and go back outside.

And then, as I'm just getting my gardening gloves on, I hear another loud scream from Neddie. Okay, now I'm really furious! Jason is going to get it this time!

This is a common problem! When I was approached with the opportunity to join a parent study group, I jumped at the chance. Jason and Neddie seemed to be in conflict all the time and I just didn't know what to do. Punishing certainly wasn't working. I couldn't separate them all the time and the situation seemed to be getting worse. I changed my approach by beginning to put into practice some of the helpful tips I was learning and it was magical how the kids' behavior changed.

First, you must realize that **the children's fighting belongs to *them.*** It is their business. "Whoa!" you might say, "I don't want them to hurt each other!" What you'll find is that if you **ignore the fighting** it will gradually lessen. Any bruises or cuts that result are usually not life-threatening. Also, if they don't want to be hurt, they won't fight.

How do you know who started it? You don't. You have no business interfering because you don't have all the facts. It's best to wait it out and ignore it. When they come to you to settle it, say in a calm, cool tone, "I'm sure you can handle this yourselves." Then turn away and go on with what you were doing. **If they get no attention for fighting, it will gradually stop. But you must balance the scales by giving them lots of attention when they're getting along.**

What I discovered about my own situation was that the younger one, Neddie, was provoking Jason until Jason reacted with a slap or a poke. Neddie would then scream, I would run in, blame Jason, and cuddle Neddie. Poor Jason very often got punished as well and our relationship had deteriorated as a result. When I stopped reacting and interfering, Neddie stopped getting attention for his misbehavior. My relationship with Jason improved tremendously, especially when I consciously began to encourage him, recognizing all the things he did that were positive.

REMINDERS:

- ✓ Ignore fighting and arguing between children. They can handle it themselves
- ✓ You don't have the information to referee. You don't have all of the facts
- ✓ Use encouragement to balance the scale. Give attention when kids cooperate

CHAPTER SEVEN

How to Solve Eating Problems

Food is another area where many parents have difficulties with their kids. Sometimes the difficulties are caused initially by the parents themselves. Other times the problems arise as a form of attention-getting. In some cases, there is a physical root that needs to be investigated by a doctor.

I know from personal experience how upsetting kids' eating problems can be. I also know how satisfying it is to overcome them. With a definite plan to follow, you can be successful too!

When Patti was thirty-nine, after many years of trying to conceive, she and Jim were thrilled to learn that a daughter was on the way. Their baby, Kristi, was a lovely little girl with picture book looks and an easygoing personality. Imagine their dismay when, as a toddler, Kristi started to have eating problems such as sitting at meals without touching her food and refusing all efforts to persuade her to eat. Patti tried everything she could to solve the situation from bribing Kristi with treats to withholding dessert. She tried making Kristi sit at the table for long periods of time until she ate something. Mealtimes became a battleground that sometimes resulted in tears for everyone. Because Kristi wouldn't eat at mealtime, Patti carried snacks in her bag to give Kristi when she was hungry. All kinds of crackers, raisins, cereal, and fruit wrapped in attractive little packages went along on all their outings and were offered to Kristi throughout the day. Patti became increasingly worried, and without realizing it she piled food on Kristi's plate in bigger and bigger portions. Food became the biggest focus of every day and the biggest frustration.

This is a situation that many parents face on a day-to-day basis in one form or another. What can parents do to successfully change their child's relationship with food?

First, **food is served only at mealtimes.** How can a child be hungry at dinner if she snacks all afternoon?

Second, **develop a meal schedule for the family, as part of a routine that you plan for daily life.** Plan regular hours for meals and try for at least one where the family can sit down together. No food is offered in between meals. Children do not need to be fed every one or two hours. Remember the schedule your child had as a baby? Babies are usually fed every three to four hours. Many parents offer food as a way to keep children from misbehaving—have toys or books available instead.

If a child starts to have problems with food, often a new baby has entered the family or something has happened to shift attention away from him. Perhaps he's started daycare, or there's a new nanny, or some similar life change has occurred. As well, parents might have their own views of what amounts and foods children *should* eat and impose their ideas on the kids. When parents start to obsess, kids will react by resisting. Another place where democracy can solve the problem!

There is tremendous security for kids in a daily routine that can be flexible at times but is "written in stone" as much as possible. Even if you have an erratic work schedule, you must develop a regular schedule for your family. **Children who have a daily routine feel safer, more secure, and more settled.** As a result, they are calmer because they know what to expect as their day unfolds.

Third, **offer a selection of healthy foods at the table for the entire family. Let your child choose the items he wants.** If there are raw and cooked vegetables available in separate dishes and plates of beef or chicken, for example, he can choose what he'd like to eat. Because he hasn't snacked all afternoon, he will likely be hungry and reach out to pick something to eat. Once kids are on a normal diet, they no longer need "special" foods or servings unless there is a medical issue. They enjoy eating like the rest of the family.

Fourth, **do not help and do not talk about it. Remove the food from the table when the rest of the family is finished** without making any comments about what your picky eater has consumed. If broccoli isn't eaten, ignore it. You may remember how you yourself had foods that you didn't like as a child.

Many times the child with the eating challenges may become the center of attention at the family table, with everyone focused on what she has or hasn't eaten. She soon realizes that Mom and Dad pay more attention to her than to anyone else at dinner. She has become the star of the show. By ignoring her attempts to gain attention with food-related complaints, the family helps her to look for more positive ways of getting their attention. It's very important that all members of the family, plus nannies and babysitters, are taught this, and parents need to remember to **give encouragement for all her positive behavior.**

"Mom, I don't like this! I hate egg sandwiches!" said Joey at lunchtime as he pushed his plate away. His mother did not respond and wouldn't be tempted to comment. She talked about the day, the weather, and asked what Joey did at kindergarten that morning. When she was finished eating, she cleared the table. About two hours later, Joey asked for a snack, complaining that he was hungry. "I'm sorry you're feeling hungry, Joey," she said in a friendly way. "Dinner is at 6:00 pm."

It's crucial that you stay loving and friendly when children suffer the results of their choices. Joey chose not to eat lunch. When he became hungry, his mom didn't say, "I told you so!" She was **training** Joey, not manipulating him.

Food is an important part of many cultures. Some mothers regularly make special meals for certain members of the family. If you are from this kind of background, it will be harder for you to stay focused on helping your child to eat only at mealtime and eat what the rest of the family eats. If you can make a start and stick with it, you'll be training your child to eat properly for the rest of his life.

REMINDERS:

✓ Develop a meal schedule for the family and stick to it as much as possible

✓ Offer a selection of foods that the family can choose from at the table

✓ Do not coax, remind, pressure, or bribe your picky eaters. Ignore the lack of eating

✓ Food is served only at mealtimes

✓ When the child is hungry after refusing food at mealtime, he waits until the next meal to eat

✓ Remove food from the table after the rest of the family is finished eating

✓ Dessert is not a reward. It is part of the meal. Don't punish by withholding dessert

✓ Remember to give encouragement for all positive behavior

✓ If food is served to the picky eater, make portions very small. She can ask for more

CHAPTER EIGHT

What to do About Temper Tantrums

You may sometimes see young children having temper tantrums in the shopping mall, or a teenager yelling and even swearing at her parents. It's embarrassing when it happens in public, and it is extremely discouraging when it happens on a regular basis at home. Why does this happen, and what can be done about it?

In the case of older children, their relationships with parents may be almost nonexistent except for orders from the parents and resistance from the kids. Sincere communication has stopped long before this point. If you can have a meaningful conversation with your teen, you can explore reasons for rude behavior and you both can express your feelings, coming to a mutual conclusion. If this isn't possible, counseling is recommended. **It is so important to keep communication avenues open with your kids, starting from when they are very young.**

Sometimes children "hit the wall" because of being overtired or overstimulated. Being sensitive to their signals of fatigue and going home from an outing before they get too tired is one way to prevent tantrums. **But many temper tantrums occur because of parental inconsistency and lack of planning.**

Henry, four, was used to getting his own way. Jill, a single mom and busy lawyer, felt stretched between balancing her career and spending time with Henry. She thought she needed to spend more time with him and she constantly had a nagging feeling of guilt. When she was at home with Henry, she gave in to his increasing commands for attention in order to please him. As a result, Henry grew bossier and demanding, and Jill often felt drained by his behavior.

It was Saturday afternoon and Jill had to get some food shopping done before dinnertime. "Would you like to go to the grocery store, Henry?" asked Jill. "No," Henry replied. He was deeply engrossed with his blocks. Jill waited for half an hour and asked Henry again. "We really need to go soon, Henry," she said. Again he refused to go. Finally, feeling pushed for time, Jill stood up and announced that it was time to go. She got Henry's jacket and tried to put it on him. He resisted, threw himself on the floor and yelled, "No! No! No!" He writhed around on the floor while Jill tried to get him up. Finally, she was able to pick him up and carry him to the car where she fought him into his car seat. At the checkout counter at the store, Henry reached for a package of candies. When Jill took them away and put them back, Henry screamed and cried. Embarrassed at the attention they were getting from onlookers, Jill gave him the candies and checked out her groceries. She fell into her seat in the car feeling defeated and hopeless.

Jill is caught in a situation where she allows a four year old to be in charge. She needs to realize that she must **take control, make the major decisions, and put a home routine in place** that will serve both her and Henry. Henry is on a strict schedule at school and daycare and needs structure at home as well. With a framework of a **solid routine** that includes mealtime, bedtime, playtime, grocery shopping, and so on, he will feel secure, knowing what to expect in his day. Jill needs to work out the routine and let Henry know the details in a friendly way.

Henry learned that his powerful behavior gets him anything he wants, especially his mother's full attention. Jill must come to terms with her feelings of guilt, even if she goes for some counseling, because they are the root of the inconsistent way she deals with Henry. When it's time to go shopping (her decision, not his, and part of the routine), she should give him five minutes' notice in a friendly way, perhaps setting a timer so the timer tells them when to go. If she likes, she can enlist his help in setting the timer as one way to prepare him and keep her composure.

She then can offer him a choice of which jacket or sweater he'll wear. The choice is not whether to go or not, but **how** they will go. Henry can choose to go the long way or the short way to the store, for example. If a treat is allowed, this is discussed ahead of time and Henry knows what his choices are. Jill must **be consistent** so Henry knows his limits.

Above all, Jill must **ignore temper tantrums.** She simply must not respond, but walk away. When the tantrum winds down from her lack of attention, she can return. **She must not talk about it**, taking no notice of it whatsoever. Giving attention to such misbehavior only reinforces it. In the store, she can withdraw and look everywhere but at her child. On the other hand, she needs to recognize Henry's positive behavior in times when he is not demanding and overbearing.

When he is behaving acceptably she must notice and comment with a positive remark such as, "It's so much fun to be with you, Henry!" or, "I enjoy your company, honey." Henry will gradually shift to more acceptable behavior that gives him the attention he needs.

By ignoring temper tantrums completely and balancing this with encouragement for your child's good behavior, temper tantrums will cease because they aren't gaining the intended result: your attention.

REMINDERS:

- ✓ Keep communication lines open with all ages. With older kids, sit down and discuss the situation, finding out what they're thinking and explaining your position. It's possible to reach a mutual conclusion in a friendly way
- ✓ Temper tantrums often occur when small kids are tired or hungry
- ✓ Parents must put in place a routine for meals, bedtime, shopping, etc. and stick to it so kids know what to expect
- ✓ Children need to know ahead of time what treats they can have on shopping trips
- ✓ Tantrums should be ignored. Walk away and return when it's over
- ✓ No matter what the age of the child, give lots of attention for positive behavior, not for misbehavior

CHAPTER NINE

How to Handle Sleeping Problems

There are a variety of issues with children's bedtime and sleep patterns that can leave you exhausted and irritable. For instance, do you dread the bedtime routine because you have trouble getting the kids to go to bed at night? **One of the most prevalent problems is setting a bedtime, sticking to it, and getting children to go to bed without an argument.**

Amy, five, refused to get ready for bed. She wanted to stay up and play with her dolls and ignored her mother's signals that it was bedtime. Finally, her father bellowed at her and carried her to her room while she sobbed and resisted. Bedtimes were becoming a real battle.

Lack of routine could be at the root of the above scenario. Amy needs to know her bedtime. This can be done by teaching her what bedtime looks like on the clock. If she has a warning of ten minutes before bedtime, she'll be more prepared to stop playing. A timer could signal the time that she has to leave and go to her bedroom. Also, **if bedtime is a pleasant experience, with a story and a talk about her day, she'll be more likely to want to go and get ready.**

Jeffrey didn't want to go for his nap. Kate, his mom, remained cool and calm. She took him by the hand and asked him how he'd like to go upstairs. "Do you want to sing the ABCs or count, Jeffrey?" she asked playfully. "Let's sing the ABCs, Mommy," said Jeffrey. They went upstairs joyfully singing the ABC song and Jeffrey hopped onto his bed. "I love you, sweetie," said Kate as she tucked him in and gave him a kiss.

Kate remained friendly even though Jeffrey was resistant at first. Nap time was not negotiable but she gave him a choice of **how** to go for his nap. She engaged his attention, made it fun, and refused to get into a power struggle situation by ordering him to go upstairs.

If your child has problems with sleep, chances are that you aren't getting your sleep either.

Trevor and Chris were suffering from lack of sleep. They were so tired that they could barely get up in the morning and found themselves yawning at work and even nodding off at their desks at times. Several times during the night, Beatrice, three, and Kelly, five, were coming into their bedroom wanting attention of some kind. Trevor would get up, then Chris, to get drinks of water or keep them company until they settled. Because they were so tired they sometimes allowed the children to come into their bed. This soon became a solid habit that cost them their rest because of broken sleep and lack of room in the bed.

How would you solve the above problem? This is a place where **training is key**. You can **state what you will do.** Simply tell the children that you will no longer get up in the night to answer their calls. They need to know that you need your sleep and will not accept being called in the middle of the night. Then follow through. **Shut your door and lock it if need be. Do not answer calls.**

You may feel there is a safety issue here. If your child is ill, you should be available, but sometimes your availability continues long after the illness has ended. The first night you talk about the situation and state that you will no longer be getting up when they call and will see them in the morning.

There may be knocking on your bedroom door. Instead of ordering them back to bed, say nothing and wait. They may try again a few times but will usually give up. Some parents have found a child asleep outside their door in the morning. **Don't feel sorry for them.** Your own health is at stake as well as theirs. It may take only one night to train children to respect rest time and the whole family will benefit.

When "good nights" were said and the light was turned off, Barry, six, hardly waited two minutes before he called for a drink of water. His dad took him a drink and said good night again. A few minutes later, Barry appeared, saying he couldn't find his teddy bear. This time his mom went in, found the bear, and went back to sit down with her book. After four or five times of going in to settle Barry, his dad finally warned him not to bother them again. Barry didn't stop repeating this behavior until he was yelled at and threatened with punishment.

Barry's parents need to train him to stay in bed and go to sleep. When he is in bed and kissed good night, they tell him that they'll see him in the morning. When he comes out of his room with requests, they go on reading or watching TV and ignore him. They pretend that he's in his bed and don't answer him. If Barry has had a story read to him, has been tucked in, and given a kiss good night, he learns by his parents' actions that no more attention is available to him afterward. His parents don't need to give orders. **They have stated what they will do in a friendly manner and they stick to it.**

Remember that kids get mistaken ideas about the attention they deserve. Often it isn't even a conscious decision to misbehave to get that attention. As a parent you need to look at why they might be wanting such attention. Do they think a brother or sister is preferred? Are you giving enough encouragement when they behave properly? Remain loving and friendly at all costs and **do not give in, even once, to negative behavior** or you'll have to start all over again.

REMINDERS:

✓ Bedtime problems often occur from a lack of a consistent routine

✓ Spending some time reading a story and talking about the day helps children settle down for the night

✓ Giving a choice of *how* to go to bed (counting, saying ABCs, etc.) gives a child some input into the decision to go to bed

✓ Train your kids to stay in their beds and not come into yours

✓ Bedtime attention-getting has a cause. Find out what it is and act on it

CHAPTER TEN

How to Stop Excessive Attention-Getting

When you find yourself annoyed by your child's attempts to get your attention, **stop and ask yourself what might be going on.** Is she getting tons of your attention but still demanding more? Or do you think she might be discouraged, feeling that she is being left out somehow? No matter what may be the cause, she might attempt to get attention through a multitude of acts that immediately focus your eyes and ears on her. She could be bothering you when you're on the phone, pulling at your pant leg when you're busy, talking loudly when you're in conversation with someone, picking her nose, swearing, dawdling, or, as babies and toddlers often do, getting into "off-limit" areas of your home. **Most of the time this behavior doesn't arise from a conscious decision, but from a deep need to belong.** Or, as in the following case of Brenda, she thinks you belong only to her.

> *Brenda, four, is an only child to parents who know they won't have more children. Rex and Nancy, her parents, work outside their home all day and Brenda was placed in daycare from infancy. Now that she's older, Brenda has started school as well. Rex and Nancy are devoted parents, wanting to raise Brenda in the best way possible. They think that spending all their time with her from the time they get home until she goes to bed is the best way to do this. Every spare moment that he has after work, Rex spends playing with Brenda. Nancy focuses on Brenda's meals, wanting her to have nutritious, healthy food. Brenda has developed a sense of entitlement toward her parents and acts like she believes that they're there to serve her. When other people are present, Brenda interrupts the conversation. When she is not noticed, she talks very loudly and quickly to drown out what is being said. She gives orders to Nancy when she wants something and sometimes is verbally abusive to her when she doesn't get her way.*

Rex and Nancy have a child who believes she is the center of the world. Unless they begin to train her otherwise, she'll become more and more self-centered and tyrannical. They must sit down with Brenda and discuss an evening routine with her. They map out times for themselves to relax after work, and time for playing with Brenda. At bedtime, they make sure to plan time to read to her and cuddle her. On the weekend when they're all home, they plan play time with her and possibly play dates with friends her age. The routine may contain errands and shopping as well. Brenda's time to play alone is included and discussed with her. She needs to be able to entertain herself without depending on parental involvement; her parents need a break as well.

Here a timer could be used with Brenda, so she knows when to join her parents after her time alone. When Brenda wants more attention at first, her parents let her know that they're busy with other things and point out the time they'll play with her, ignoring the pressure of her demanding behavior. It may take a few days before she realizes that she can't run the show, but **with consistent application of routine, the whole family will become happier.** Rex and Nancy, finally having some time to themselves, will become more relaxed and enjoy their daughter's company without feeling burdened.

Since too much attention-seeking is antisocial, it can be very upsetting and embarrassing. How can such irritating behavior be stopped in its tracks? There are two actions you must take: **give your child attention when it's appropriate** and **ignore her efforts to engage you when the time isn't right.**

Will it take a lot of effort on your part to turn things around? Of course! But it's worth it. **It takes resolve, patience,** and **consistency.**

It seemed that every time Patti turned around, Oliver was picking his nose. When she noticed it, she would raise her voice and order him to stop. It got so that she began to dislike him and didn't want to be near him and his dirty fingers.

If she stops to think about it, Patti could likely see that instead of helping Oliver stop picking his nose, she's making the situation worse. Looking closely, we see that **Oliver has lost the positive attention he seeks but has his mom fully engaged when his finger is in his nose.** Patti needs to hug and kiss her son when his hands are clean, for example, after a bath or after washing up before dinner. She could spend extra time with him at bedtime, reading to him and talking about his day. She needs to tell him how she loves him and focus on encouraging him for anything positive that he does during the day. When he picks his nose, she must turn her back, possibly leave the room, and say nothing. Ignoring his offensive behavior, Patti must balance the scales with encouragement and love in times when Oliver isn't nose-picking.

It seemed that every time Carol got on the phone, her two-year-old Melanie would cause a commotion. Whether she was at home or out at the park, the minute Carol got on the phone Melanie would want to climb on her knee. Often Melanie would open the kitchen cupboards and take out pots and pans, banging them loudly. When Carol couldn't hear, she would yell at Melanie to stop, interrupting her conversation many times to say, "Stop it, Melanie! Mommy is on the phone!" When Melanie continued her attention-getting, Carol would reluctantly have to end the conversation.

Melanie is asking for needed attention, and Carol may sometimes interrupt her time with Melanie to answer the phone or make a call. If Carol is playing with or is reading Melanie a story, she needs to give Melanie her full attention. She can ignore the ringing of the phone and let it go to voicemail, calling back when Melanie naps or is settled with her toys. If she spends some time with Melanie before she makes a call, it's likely that Melanie will continue to play quietly by herself and won't need to demand more attention. If an important call is expected, Carol can explain that she must take it and will return to play in a few minutes. If Melanie starts interrupting, she can ignore Melanie's efforts to get attention and go to another room to take the call. **The key here is to respect your child by not interrupting your special time with her. Ignore any attempts to get your attention when it isn't warranted.**

There can be different reasons for excessive demands for attention. Look carefully at the dynamics of your family, your own habits, and the needs of your child. Is everyone happy? If not, there are reasons that will emerge when you examine the situation and there are ways to solve the problem.

REMINDERS:

- ✓ If you feel you spend enough time with your child and still have problems with excessive attention-getting, stop and consider the root of the issue
- ✓ Your child may be discouraged about her place in the family and subconsciously is reaching out for validation
- ✓ Putting a routine in place that covers family times for work and play and sticking to it consistently is a way that can help all members of the family
- ✓ Bedtime is a very important time for giving encouragement and attention to your kids
- ✓ Bad habits like nose-picking can arise from a need for positive attention from parents
- ✓ Ignore bad habits by turning your back or leaving the room. Balance this by giving love and encouragement at other times
- ✓ When playing with your kids, turn off your phone. Respect them by giving them your full attention

CHAPTER ELEVEN

What to do About Talking Back and Saying No

A child who talks back is a child who thinks he is in charge. How does it happen that he gets to the point that he refuses to cooperate with the people who love him more than anything else?

One cause of this problem could be that parents are extremely busy people. They have a time challenge and may have lost patience with their child for some reason, perhaps because of his misbehavior or undue attention-getting. They may talk to their child and end up giving orders instead of inspiring their child's cooperation. If this is sounds like what is happening to you, backing up and taking a hard look at your priorities and your life schedule is step one.

Secondly, **listen to yourself when you talk to your child.** He may be mimicking your own tone. He could feel discouraged and lost in the rush of the day. If you start to **consciously encourage him, ignoring his back talk and attention-getting,** you'll build a better relationship with him from the ground up. This may take some time, but you'll be surprised how **he'll change and become easier to get along with when he feels more valued by you.**

If you're not sure how to encourage him, go to Chapter Three for a review. You may want to re-read that chapter many times because **positive encouragement is a skill that is so important and so crucial to your child's feeling of value that it must be at the front of your mind as much as possible.**

Another reason that a child could talk back could be that she is a powerful child who usually gets her way and feels she is more important than you.

Jemma, seven, was a very bright girl who had her parents, Judy and Larry, wrapped around her little finger. She was allowed to have her way most of the time. But when she was refused Jemma would verbally abuse Judy or Larry until there was a yelling match. "I hate you!" she would often shout and her parents would back down, feeling hurt and angry. When they asked her to do something, she would say "No!" Her lack of respect was driving them crazy.

Judy and Larry had been attending a parenting course and decided to act on this problem. They began to see that they had abandoned their roles as heads of the household and were intimidated by their child. Jemma sensed their hesitation and stepped forward to take the position of boss.

In the course on parenting, Judy and Larry learned that they must not be afraid to say no to Jemma. They had to reclaim their position as leaders and teachers. When Jemma asked for something inappropriate, they could explain their refusal and consistently not back down.

They were in charge and they would not give in to her demands. They needed to be aware that Jemma needed limits and structure to feel secure and that she would be a happier child if they took control. To balance this new behavior on their part, lots of encouragement needed to be given to Jemma when she was cooperative, and recognition of any positive behavior was crucial.

When Jemma talked back to them, Judy and Larry learned to turn away from her, perhaps even leaving the room. When she cooperated, they gave her their full attention. They also realized they were role models and changed their manner of speaking to Jemma, using a neutral tone and not reacting when they felt hurt by her.

At quiet times when everyone felt good about each other, Judy and Larry talked to Jemma about the need to respect other people. Gradually, as Judy and Larry grew more confident in standing up to Jemma, and as she started to realize her limits, Jemma began to act more respectfully toward her parents.

When you're speaking with a friend and find that he's been distracted by something or someone and is no longer listening to you, how do you feel? He may look away from you, glance around the room at other people, and you realize that you're not being heard. You then do a swift about-turn, perhaps changing the subject to regain his attention. The same principle operates when talking with your child. **If he's talking back to you, withdraw and look elsewhere or leave the room. You can make the following statement, and make it once only, "I don't listen to children who talk that way."**

Then you **follow through** and when your child is rude again you turn away without talking about it or showing that you're hurt. You turn away not in anger, but quietly and with a sense of detachment. Your child soon realizes that his rudeness has no effect and he chooses a more respectful way of talking, which gains your attention. **It's crucial that you never notice his rudeness again.** You simply withdraw in a neutral way. **But remember to notice and respond to respectful, positive behavior whenever it occurs. Listen for it and acknowledge it. Notice positives and ignore negatives.**

You may forget and resort to your old parenting ways once in a while, especially at the beginning. You're learning and it's okay. Just dust yourself off and start again. It gets easier with time.

REMINDERS:

✓ Listen to yourself when you talk to your kids. Do you give orders? They may be copying you

✓ Put a schedule in place that gives you time to spend with your children

✓ Ignore children talking back by stating *once only* that you don't listen to kids who talk like that, then *turn away* when it happens, perhaps leaving the room

✓ Be sure to give lots of encouragement for positive behavior. Re-read Chapter Three to make sure you know how to do this

✓ Notice all positives. Ignore negative behavior

CHAPTER TWELVE

Great Communication: How to Get Your Child to Talk to You

"How was school today, John?"
"Okay."
"What did you do today?"
"Nothing much."

The above exchange with a child is unbelievably common. We want to talk with him but don't know how to avoid one-syllable answers. What a treat it is when he opens up and tells us his feelings and inner thoughts! Often we know nothing about our child's day from the time he leaves home in the morning until he returns after school. When we ask, he thinks we're prying, especially if he's a preteen or teenager.

We parents are busy people and our children are busy too. Because of this, days will go by without any meaningful communication between us, unless we decide to give communication top priority and learn how to make it more satisfying. Confronted with a beautiful, special human being who we love very much but have lost touch with, **we can become frustrated and even give up the effort to reach him.** The result is that he thinks we don't care and don't want to talk. The situation snowballs until we're almost strangers.

We communicate most with our children when they're babies. We spend hours teaching them to talk. As they grow more independent from us, we talk with them less and less. As more children join the family and demand our attention the way that babies do, the older child is thought to be able to get along on his own and in fact can get on by himself in many ways.

We forget to sit and enjoy him perhaps because our days are full of other things. When he becomes a teenager and we want to know what he's thinking, we finally try to talk to him with little success. If you have this issue going on in your family, how do you change it? How do you get your kids to talk to you?

If you can, start early when children do nothing but talk. You can establish times when conversation flows easily and you develop an easygoing routine for communication. The best time to begin is when your child starts to talk. **Bedtime is a**

wonderful occasion for closeness, starting with story time and evolving into talks about the day.

Jeannie, five, and Peter, seven, loved bedtime. From the time they were much smaller, it was a time when Mom or Dad read stories to them after they had brushed their teeth and finished their bedtime routine. It was also a time when they could talk about what had happened that day at school and in the neighborhood. Mom and Dad encouraged them by starting sentences with "Tell me about . . ." and open-ended questions such as "What happened when . . . ?" They avoided questions that could be answered with "yes" or "no." They developed a routine of asking about the best things that happened to them that day and the worst things.

If the subject progressed to talking about feelings, a sense of real intimacy grew between them with comments like, "Tell me how you felt about . . ." Mom and Dad listened carefully, giving the kids their full attention. If the phone rang, they let it go to voicemail. They showed the kind of respect for the children that they expected for themselves, as no one likes to be interrupted when speaking. This mutual respect established a pattern of good communication that established a relationship that continued into and past the children's teenage years.

With an older child or teen, the best idea is not to ask direct questions but to make yourself available to him by simply being in the same room with him. You could watch TV together and ask his opinion on the program. **Listen to what he says, being open and friendly. Avoid criticism and preaching. Be nonjudgmental.** His ideas will be different from yours. If he finds you accept his ideas, he'll likely want to share them with you again.

You also might ask permission to sit on his bed and invite his opinion about something such as a choice you're facing at work or a small challenge that came up during your day.

Kids love to give advice and, if you sincerely ask for help, they'll try to assist you and likely will come up with amazingly good solutions. This can turn into a two-way exchange if, for example, you ask, **"What was the best thing that happened to you today?"** or "What kinds of problems did you have today?" If they invite you to play a game on the computer or another activity, make time to do so. The closeness that develops from sharing time can be a starting point for older children and teens to tell you about their friends or life at school.

If your children are involved in clubs or activities at school, you can start discussions with them about the things that interest them. Sometimes the best opportunity arises when you're driving them to a team practice or music lesson. "What do you like best about your sport, your music lesson, your music teacher, etc.?" you could ask.

When you ask that particular question, you'll often hear about what they don't like or are having trouble with. A car ride could also be a time when you ask for their advice. Make sure that it's a topic that's appropriate—avoid making them into confidants about heavy issues in your life. **Really listen and don't interrupt. Don't let the telephone break the spell. Be sure to tell them how much you enjoy their company and their help.**

Have you thought of taking one of your children out somewhere on her own? If you take her out to lunch, for example, she feels special and the occasion may provoke good conversation.

Look at your child when she talks. Concentrate on what she's saying and answer thoughtfully and respectfully.

You might have a seriously discouraged child who won't talk with you at all. If you're in this predicament, **take time to analyze what could be wrong in his life.** You may need to talk with a counselor at school to find out if your child is having trouble in some way, either academically or socially. If you think that the root of the trouble could be in your home, in your relationship with him, for instance, or if he is the middle child and feels that the other children are preferred, you have the ability to turn things around.

I've had personal experience with a child who felt his brother was the preferred one, and that he just couldn't win. What I did was to go to his room when he ran there crying one day. I sat on his bed. He was very tense and pulled away and faced the wall. I said, "I know that you think I love your brother more than you." "Yes, you do, Mom," he cried and started to sob. "I love you just as much as Neddie, honey," I said. "I've made some serious mistakes in blaming you for the fighting and for other things and am beginning to take a parenting course so I can be a better mom."

I began to rub his back and ended up rocking and holding him as his whole body relaxed and he gradually stopped his crying. We talked a little about the new things I was learning and I again told him how much I loved him. This was the beginning of a new relationship with my child that continued as I learned, studied, and practiced the parenting approach I'm writing about. You can turn your situation around, too.

REMINDERS:

- ✓ Don't give up when your child refuses to talk. Analyze what could be wrong in his life
- ✓ If he's older, make yourself available to him by watching a TV program and asking for his opinion, etc. Don't be judgmental, but listen carefully. Avoid criticism
- ✓ Use the time driving the kids places to ask them about their day in open-ended questions such as, "What was the best thing about your day?" or "What do you like about your music or swimming lesson, etc.?"
- ✓ Listen, listen, and listen
- ✓ When kids are young, bedtime is important for closeness and communication. Start early to read bedtime stories and cuddle

CHAPTER THIRTEEN

Messy Bedrooms and Family Spaces: Getting Kids to Clean Up

Kendra, fourteen, and her mom, Cheryl, are at war over Kendra's bedroom. Cheryl and Kendra once had fun picking out colors for the bedroom walls and getting lovely new bed linens. Now Cheryl can't pass the doorway to Kendra's room without seething inside and making caustic comments when she sees the clothing on the floor, the unmade bed, and the other clutter. Seeing the new duvet in a pile on the floor sets her teeth on edge to the point that her jaw aches. Cheryl just doesn't know how to make Kendra keep her room tidy. Her anger and Kendra's resistance are careening toward a power struggle that could last throughout Kendra's teenage years.

Why do children's messy rooms bother parents so much? It could be that the rooms are a highly visible example that they aren't in complete control of the kids and therefore are less than perfect parents. When there's a high standard of cleanliness and order in the home especially, it's very hard to take when it doesn't extend to the kids' rooms.

No matter what age children are, there's usually a problem around neatness and order. In some families there's constant, futile arguing as parents endlessly nag at their kids to be tidier. Sometimes parents simply give up and pick up after the children themselves. This teaches kids to expect their parents to serve them.

Tidiness can be motivated with training that can be started when a child is very young. Picking up toys together at the end of the day builds a good foundation. This is especially true if it's done with a happy atmosphere, even made into a game, rather than ordering kids to do it themselves. Helping to keep a bedroom neat by organizing storage areas and shelves is fundamental, too. Some kids have mountains of toys that make clean up time discouraging. Toys could be rotated not just for easier pick up, but to maintain children's interest. **Parents who want tidy kids must set a good example of tidiness themselves.** Children model their behavior based on what they see their parents do.

Attention-getting children might find that by being messy they can keep their parents busy with them. Their parents' nagging is the payoff—the child's reassurance that they are being noticed. If your child feels out of place in the family group, that another child gets more attention, she'll look for a way to get the attention she wants by misbehaving. This is most often not a conscious decision. If you're passionate about neatness, she can get you to notice her by being messy. The more you talk about it, the more you inspire the cycle of bad reaction. By ignoring her messiness, but encouraging other things she does that are positive, the messy behavior will melt away.

In Chapter One, I talked about Alfred Adler's view that children and parents are all deserving of dignity and respect, and that we need to see our children as equals. What would happen if we thought of a child's room as his own space to keep as he desired, and we kept out of it? General cleaning schedules would still apply as we see in the example that follows.

Julie, her husband Bill, and Skye, ten, sat down and formulated a plan together about cleaning Skye's bedroom. They all felt that her bedroom was her private space and that parents shouldn't impose their standards of neatness on her room. They also agreed that the whole house had to be cleaned regularly for health reasons. The three of them laid down some ground rules together about how to keep Skye's room clean. Every week, on Friday, the house was vacuumed and dusted. Saturday was laundry day. Julie and Bill helped Skye to see that her room couldn't be dusted or cleaned if the floor was littered with her things and if her clothes weren't in the laundry hamper, they couldn't be washed.

Skye had a good relationship with her parents and felt valued by being involved with setting up the schedule. She could keep her room the way she wanted, but had to clean up once a week. It was decided that Julie or Bill could remind her the day before cleaning and laundry days. The rest was up to her. She had the choice to pick up her things or let someone else do it. If she forgot to put her dirty clothes in the laundry hamper, they weren't washed. If there were still clothes or books on the floor on cleaning day, they'd be put into a bag in the storage closet.

When her favorite jeans missed the wash the first time, Skye remembered to put them in the hamper the following week. When she had to go to the storage room to a bag and look for her library book, she remembered to clear up the floor before cleaning day the next week. It didn't take long for Skye to realize that it was her responsibility to look after her room. Julie and Bill kept a friendly attitude, didn't criticize or nag, and allowed Skye to experience the results of her own actions. She was allowed to keep her bedroom the way she wanted between cleanings.

If you decide to let your child experience the consequences of his own choice, **you must keep a friendly attitude. No criticism must be voiced.** By setting up the scenario ahead of time, hopefully with his input, you put his room into his own hands. **Kids can have choices regarding their rooms but those choices have to be made within the limits of a family routine.**

The same strategy can be employed regarding family rooms, entry halls, mudrooms, etc. The night before cleaning day, notice is given that vacuuming and dusting will take place the next day. If things are left around when it comes time to clean, they are put into a bag or box in the basement or storage area. No talking about it is necessary. The kids don't like searching for their things and will soon learn to put them away when the cleaning warning is given.

When you no longer nag or give orders, the atmosphere of the family changes. Don't forget to recognize your kids' acts of cooperation and contribution, small though they may be. When you encourage them, you build trust and mutual support.

REMINDERS:

- ✓ Tidiness can begin when kids are very young. Develop a routine of picking up toys at the end of the day and make it a game
- ✓ Parents are role models for kids. Be tidy and the kids will likely follow unless they're attention-getting by being messy (go to Chapter Ten for a review of how to handle this)
- ✓ Your child's room is her space. Let her keep it the way she wants and don't impose your idea of cleanliness on her. Use your routine of vacuuming and laundry to help her clean her room at least once a week
- ✓ Families need to sit down together to draw up a routine. If kids have input, they own the routine too and there's a better chance that they'll follow it
- ✓ Remain friendly at all times when discussing kids' rooms. Let your cleaning routine be the bad guy
- ✓ Give kids a heads up before cleaning or laundry day. If they choose to ignore the warning, act accordingly without malice or saying, "I told you so"
- ✓ Don't give orders. Watch your tone of voice. Stay calm

CHAPTER FOURTEEN

How to Motivate Your Child to Help Around the House

Scott entered the family room and surveyed the mess of teen magazines, stuffed animals, and toy cars that covered the floor. He and Dorrie, his wife, had spent all day Saturday cleaning the house. His frustration had reached a point where he exploded and yelled at the kids to clean up the place or there would be no movie that night. The three children responded with angry looks and in exaggerated slow motion began to pick up their things.

If you're doing all the work around the house while your kids are playing video games, you will likely start to feel a slow burn of resentment that could end up being just plain anger. **How do you stimulate children to *want* to help out? How do you encourage their cooperation?**

It may sound impossible, but it can be done. First, you must remember that **everyone in the family deserves dignity and respect—including you.** Will you receive it if you're ordering the kids around or yelling at them for being selfish? Who wants to help a dictator who gives commands and punishes when he's not obeyed? **Acting powerful is not an option if you want to stimulate help and assistance.**

The underlying thought behind all of your actions as a parent must be that you and your children are equal. Because you are all human beings, you all deserve to be treated with consideration. When you speak to them, you must treat them as you'd treat a friend or neighbor. (You may want to re-read Chapter One to review this foundational idea.)

A good way to begin is to get the family together around the table, perhaps after a meal where everyone has been in good spirits. You can express how you've been feeling overwhelmed and tired because there's so much to do around the house and yard. Right away your kids will start to empathize with you because you haven't done any blaming or criticizing. Someone may offer to help, followed by others who don't want to be left out.

"I'm exhausted," said Pete, who had mowed and trimmed the lawn that day and cleaned the garage. "So am I," said Betty, who had weeded the flower garden, done laundry, and made dinner. "I'm so tired that I don't think I have the

energy to do one more thing today." Julie, ten, and Mark, twelve, looked at their parents who were obviously dragging, slumping in their chairs, looking completely worn out. "Wow, Mom!" responded Julie. "Can I help you do something?" She and Mark cleared the table and came back to their parents.

"Thanks for your help, kids," said Pete. "Mom and I have reached a point where we really need some help around the house. Would you be into helping us make a list of all the jobs that have to be done to run the house and take care of the yard?" Julie and Mark started to list all the things they could think of and Betty got some paper and wrote them all down. All the jobs from greatest to smallest were on the list. Before they knew it they had a long list of chores, from cooking dinner, shopping for food, vacuuming and dusting, washing the car, to cleaning the bathrooms. "Let's add 'earning the money,'" said Betty. "And paying the bills," added Pete. "Oh, and doing the laundry!" said Betty.

"What would happen if we each chose two jobs to do this week?" asked Pete. "Okay," said Mark. "What do you want me to do?" "Why don't you choose what you'd like to do, Mark?" asked Pete. Mark chose cleaning the bathroom and doing the grocery shopping. Julie wanted to dust the furniture and load and unload the dishwasher. Betty and Pete chose earning the income, doing the laundry and vacuuming, and cooking the meals. Obviously, they also had to do the jobs that hadn't been chosen, which didn't escape the children's notice.

Because Betty had chosen to cook, she drew up the grocery list. Pete agreed to drive Mark to the supermarket that morning. Betty asked if Mark would like any tips on doing the shopping. He had been to the store with her many times and had observed her comparing prices. "No,

Mom, I can handle it," he said. He also listed the things that needed to be purchased so that he could clean the bathroom later, and Betty said she'd help him find the items he would need.

Pete and Betty hugged the kids and brightened up at the prospect of help. The children had risen to the occasion and had offered to participate in the running of their home. Each week they met as a family and had the option of choosing the jobs they'd do. This way a household job would only last for one week at a time if they so wanted.

In the above example, the children felt the exhaustion of their parents and wanted to help. Would this happen in your family? If not, approaching each child individually might be best. You could say something like, "I know I've been cranky lately, but I'm just worn out with too much to do. I'm so tired and I need some help."

Then later you could bring up the subject again, when the family is together, and arrange to have a meeting just to discuss the situation. You might start the meeting by saying something like, "We all live here and we all make the mess. What can we do to ease the load?" When all the jobs get listed, kids are usually amazed at how much it takes to run a home.

It's extremely important that you let each family member have a chance to talk without comment or criticism from anyone else. In fact, in future meetings you could let each child have a turn being the chairperson; as long as he is old enough to read and write, then he could also have a turn at being secretary, writing down the jobs and who is going to do them. This list can be posted on the fridge.

Each week another meeting is held and jobs can be changed if desired. All jobs are open to choose so that not just the "easy" jobs are offered to the kids. They then take their tasks more seriously and feel they're making a more important contribution to the family.

If your eight-year-old chooses the job of cleaning the toilets, or something equally challenging, you may think she won't know how to do it but she may have observed you doing it and know what to do on her own. Ask if your assistance is needed. When jobs are done, be sure to notice and encourage them for their efforts. **Avoid criticism.** If it's necessary to redo a job, do so without damaging the child's self-respect by correcting it when the child isn't there. Possibly your high standards can come down a notch while the kids are learning.

What happens if the jobs that are chosen by kids aren't done? **Parents must be careful not to comment or criticize.** A brother or sister might come to tell you about it and you can say, "We'll discuss it at our next meeting." When the meeting date comes, someone might say, "Geoffrey didn't clean the sinks this week. What are we going to do about it?" There could be many reasons that Geoffrey didn't do his job. He has a chance to explain himself. Did he not know how to do it and need some training? Did he have a very busy week with an overloaded schedule? Was he ill? One reason might be lack of interest and that he simply didn't feel like it. **The group, rather than just the parents, can discuss the problem and find a way to motivate a family member who hasn't done his job.**

The atmosphere of a family meeting must be friendly and loving. If there's a lot of tension in your family or a lot of fighting between the children, it will take skill and patience to handle such a meeting without turning into a boss and giving orders. If you feel a meeting is too risky at the present time, leave it until the family feels more positively toward one another. You could approach children on an individual basis instead.

Your goal is to change jobs around the house from being humdrum chores done with tension to being activities that promote a feeling of value to the family as a whole. Be sure you show your appreciation for every effort made.

REMINDERS:

- ✓ Everyone in the family deserves to be treated with dignity and respect
- ✓ You and your kids are equal. You'll get their cooperation by avoiding giving orders and acting powerful
- ✓ Stimulate help from the kids by speaking to them the way you would want to be spoken to
- ✓ If you're tired and feeling overwhelmed, tell the kids. They'll empathize and likely offer to help
- ✓ Have a family get-together to discuss what it takes to run the family home and property. Schedule weekly family discussions
- ✓ Get the kids to help make a list of jobs in the house and yard
- ✓ Let kids choose one or two jobs to do for a week
- ✓ Don't criticize, but comment on anything positive
- ✓ Remember to stay calm, loving, and encouraging

CHAPTER FIFTEEN

How to Teach Your Child to Handle Money (and Stop Bugging You for More)

"Can I have this, Mom? Aw, please? C'mon, Mom, please? Puh-lease!!!" whined eight-year-old Wayne at the check-out counter. His begging and demands were getting louder and louder, embarrassing Lila, his mother, as she put the groceries on to the counter. Finally, she couldn't stand it any longer and angrily gave in, letting Wayne have the candy that he wanted just to stop his shouting. Lila felt

humiliated. She knew she'd done the wrong thing but didn't know what else to do to put a stop to Wayne's escalating demands. She felt like a bad parent and hated all the attention she was getting from strangers in the store.

How many shopping trips turn into tension on the part of parents and whining and pressuring on the part of kids? You see it all the time. Parents say, "No," but are eventually worn down until they give in just to keep the child quiet. They're left shrugging their shoulders at the onlookers nearby and feeling inadequate at their inability to handle the situation. What is the answer to this headache of a problem?

What works here is a plan—one that can be carried through consistently every time you take kids shopping. The basis of the plan is that **you set up an orderly, fair, and regular system of giving an allowance when a child shows interest in money and begins to pester for things.** A certain day of the week is "allowance day." Circumstances, rather than age, will determine his readiness. The amount of allowance takes into account his expenses, the cost of candy and treats, and even the possibility of including a portion for saving. Small children are usually thrilled to receive less than a dollar per week for an allowance. The amount can cover the candy or treat you might presently give them at the store. Given regularly on Saturday or another specified day, it can be given so that a child can spend it on a family shopping trip. As children grow older, and depending on the lifestyle and budget of the family, kids can receive an additional amount, such as one or two dollars. With each birthday or grade at school, another dollar or two can be added until it's decided that the youngster is old enough and responsible enough to be able to receive a monthly amount to cover the cost of his school books, clothing, and entertainment. Usually, kids in high school who have received allowances from early childhood are able to make their money last the full month because they have experience in handling their finances.

This opens up a wonderful opportunity for training in the handling of finances and, if you start from day one when you give the allowance for the first time, you can also include opening a bank account where he can learn to deposit his savings portion himself. Kids love to see their savings grow. They can be encouraged to save for something they really want and their excitement builds as their account balance grows. Be sure to have a way that they can monitor it with a checkbook, or online. As your child matures, his allowance is renegotiated, depending on his needs. Monthly allowances could be given, if appropriate.

Allowances are most useful when they aren't tied to chores and aren't used as bribes. Punishing by withholding an allowance is not an effective training practice. (See Chapter Three for the basic information on the futility of punishment as a parenting method.) **Your child's allowance is his right as a family member and is a regular source of income he can depend on. It's the basis of his education in the value and handling of money and the benefits of budgeting.**

Once it's established that they receive a regular allowance, kids can be told that treats won't be given on shopping trips. **If they want to buy something, they have to have their own money with them.** You must follow through regardless of any begging that might happen. If they spend allowances in one fell swoop and don't have enough the next time you're out, they have to suffer the consequences of not being able to buy what they want at that time.

It's crucial that you handle their disappointment in a caring, friendly manner, even sympathizing with their inability to get what they want. "I'm sorry you don't have your money with you today," you can say, "I know you're disappointed." Having to do without is a great lesson and means an additional lecture isn't needed.

In order to help kids plan ahead, give them plenty of notice as to when you're going shopping. With a younger child, you could ask if she has her money with her just before leaving the house.

Above all, don't get involved with telling your child how to spend her allowance. Avoid criticizing her for errors she might make. Her tastes are vastly different from yours. In my own family my youngest kids seemed to spend their total allowance on candy. As they grew older, they bought books, magazines, or saved for toys they wanted. They learned from their successes and also their failures. Experiencing the handling of money at an early age gave the kids the background that helped them to negotiate their finances as adults. Better to make mistakes when they were children!

Occasionally, an advance on their allowance or a loan was requested to help buy something special. This was allowed taking into consideration the age of the child and the needs of the particular situation.

With an allowance system in place and used consistently and without exception, shopping trips can be fun. Your relationship with your children improves and your kids feel a great sense of accomplishment in being in charge of their finances. The result is no more pressure cooker situations at the checkout counter.

REMINDERS:

- ✓ An allowance system can prevent demands for treats at the checkout counter
- ✓ Set up the allowance system as soon as kids show interest in money and ask for toys or treats when you're shopping
- ✓ The amount of the allowance is based on the age, stage, and needs of the child
- ✓ Kids learn to handle money, budget, and save when they are given an allowance
- ✓ Allowances should never be tied to jobs and never be withdrawn as a form of punishment
- ✓ Family relationships are friendlier when an allowance system is in place

CHAPTER SIXTEEN

Tension in the Family: How to Cope with Marital Discord, Financial Problems, and Illness

Sonya's and Harold's relationship was at a breaking point. For many months they had grown further and further apart. Sonya became less communicative and Harold spent more time at the office. They were both preoccupied with their troubles and, when home with their kids, they were either silent and withdrawn or angry and aggressive. Often they lashed out at one another in front of the kids, and then went several days without speaking to each other. Barry, twelve, and Jessica, ten, had no idea what was wrong with their parents but knew that their home was full of unhappiness for some reason. Jessica became teary and babyish while Barry spent more and more time in his room.

Problems of all kinds pop up in families and they generally can be worked out. Marriage troubles, however, are at a level of difficulty that can be overwhelming—for adults and kids alike. When adults have worries they can withdraw, become silent and preoccupied, or possibly vent their frustration in angry outbursts directed at family members. The kids don't understand it and react with varying levels of attention-getting habits, or misbehavior that gets worse because their parents finally notice them and give them negative attention. The children's feelings of anxiety and insecurity add fuel to the smoldering atmosphere of worry and upset. Often, the family environment is further challenged with behavior such as fighting between the kids, back talk to parents, and angry outbursts. Because parents are angry at each other, they don't parent as a unit. It isn't long before the children learn to play one against the other to get what they want.

In a troubled family, relationships will usually improve when the kids are told something about the difficulties their parents are facing. It's crucial that a child's age and maturity are taken into consideration when discussing causes of family unrest. Kids who are kept in the dark imagine that their parents don't care about them. They often even think that they're the cause of the trouble. If punishment is frequent, that feeling is reinforced. But if a child is told, "Mom and I are having some problems we have to work out," or "Dad and I are worried about our money situation," a label is put on the tension she feels around the home. Because she knows that it's something outside her, she may become less anxious and insecure.

Parents mustn't use a child as a confidant, though, or use time with children to make accusations about the other parent. When a child knows the reason for the change in atmosphere, she begins to feel better. She may later want to know if the situation is being resolved and you must be honest. Her anxiety over your problems can be dealt with by giving her lots of love and attention. **Misbehavior should be ignored and positive behavior should always be noticed and given attention.**

Neil had been feeling very tired. His energy level had dropped and he had no appetite. Finally he went to his doctor, had some tests, and was distraught to discover he had cancer. The stress level in the family went sky-high as Neil and his wife Teresa began to deal with the terrible news. They decided they had to tell their teenagers immediately that their dad was fighting cancer. Neil wanted to be open about his condition so they decided to get the family together to talk about Neil's health and how everyone could help him cope. Teresa knew that the support of the whole family would be crucial to Neil's ability to endure the treatments prescribed by his doctor. Because the children knew what was happening, they were conscious of the need to be cooperative and helpful to their parents. The children thought of ways they could make life easier for their parents, and the situation ended up drawing the family closer together.

Children have a great capability for empathy but they have to be given the opportunity to gain the knowledge that will help them to understand. As a child becomes aware of her parents' concerns, she feels closer to her parents and her understanding can give a troubled parent a much needed lift. Parental honesty reduces the pressure to keep up a front. It results in more authentic and satisfying communication among family members which leads to increased friendliness and respect.

When marriage ends in divorce, or when a family member dies, some kids need extra help such as counseling. If the family has gone through it together, however, everybody pulls together and supports each other and they usually come through it stronger than ever.

REMINDERS:

✓ Family problems such as separation, divorce, or illness can divide a family and produce misbehavior unless handled with honesty

✓ Children, especially young ones, often feel that a problem at home is their fault and need to be reassured that it isn't so

✓ When children understand the problem they usually want to help

✓ In times of trouble kids need even more encouragement and affection

CHAPTER SEVENTEEN

Is Your Child Always Unhappy? How to Help

In many families there's one child who stands out from the others, who's got certain qualities that are vastly different from his siblings. The unhappy child fits this category.

In any family picture, Nellie, eight, always looked grumpy. Many photos showed other people in the picture looking toward her, likely trying to get her to smile. She was a child who seemed unhappy most of the time, with her lower lip stuck out and her eyes downcast. She cried easily and often. She was shy, too, and clung to her mother's side when introduced to strangers. At the slightest bump from her two older brothers, she would burst into tears and react with loud screaming. As a result, they teased her, knowing that they'd get a reaction every time. Someone would rush in to save Nellie, cuddle her, wipe away her tears, and coax her into a better mood. At school she was often picked on, ending up in the office at least once a week.

If you have a child like Nellie in your family, you probably flip-flop between feeling sorry for her and being greatly annoyed by her. Do you try to solve her problems for her? Do you interfere in her fights with her siblings, becoming the mediator who usually blames the others and hugs her until she stops crying? Sometimes you probably yell at her because you feel so helpless and incapable of figuring out how to help her become more courageous.

The majority of us would choose happiness over misery. Why does someone, even a child such as Nellie, choose a life of constant unhappiness? To answer this, we need to look at what kind of rewards come from being sad. First and foremost, when Nellie cries out, **she receives a great deal of attention.** Her cries produce immediate action from parents and other adults. Her problems are taken care of by others so she doesn't need to solve them herself. She also has a unique place in the family group. She feels special.

A child who needs to be unhappy to feel special is someone who is vastly discouraged. He doesn't have a healthy feeling of belonging to the family group. He can't get the full attention of his parents, especially if he has a younger sibling or older brothers or sisters who seem so much more able than he is. He discovers that by being weak and gloomy he can take center stage and have the recognition he couldn't get before. Often, he'll develop a victim personality, unconsciously setting himself up to be the class scapegoat or the prey of schoolyard bullies.

It's important to have a meeting at school and determine what might be happening there that might be increasing your child's insecurity and depression. You can map out a plan of action with his teacher to encourage his strong points and to play down his attempts to be pitied.

You must stop feeling sorry for him. Pity is debilitating and doesn't inspire courage. When he's hurt, you can give a quick warm hug and step back, assuring him that you know he can handle himself safely next time. **Your faith in your child will help him to cope with problems himself.** When you refuse to pity him, you strengthen him. In other words, **pay attention to his strengths. Ignore his weaknesses.**

Learn to stay out of fights among your kids (see Chapter Six for help). **Tell all the kids that you know they can solve their differences themselves.** You can say you weren't there when it happened and so can't offer your opinion about their problem. This way you don't defend one child and blame others, which can be extremely unfair. By staying out of fights and not blaming, you're encouraging friendliness and you'll find that fights happen less and less.

The next step you can take to help build confidence is to **talk with your child and help him to see that his behavior around other kids promotes aggression and that by crying, he's giving the mean kids what they want.** Help him to ignore kids while at home and at school when they provoke him, and to walk away from taunts without reacting. Recognize all his efforts to remain calm.

When you understand that your child's sadness comes from discouragement, you can actively start to encourage him (see Chapter Three for more information on how to do this). **Pay attention to your child when he's not moping. Ignore his efforts to get you to focus on him when he comes to you with tales of woe.** You can suddenly be needed somewhere else and withdraw, telling him that you're sure he can handle the problem. **Notice any positive, helpful behavior on his part. Give lots of hugs when he's not sad.**

Assess the way you treat each of your children. Are you giving equal time to them? Are you paying attention to positive, cooperative behavior? If not, a child can become discouraged, feeling that others are preferred. In that case, you can rectify the situation by changing your approach. **If you feel the problem is beyond your capability, seek help from a counselor.**

REMINDERS:

✓ A sad child causes a lot of concern at home and at school. It can be a child's unconscious way of getting attention

✓ It's crucial to understand the reasons for the sadness by talking with your child's teachers and assessing the home situation. Counseling may be needed

✓ Pay attention to his strengths. Ignore his weaknesses

✓ Talk with your child and give him attention when he's not moping

✓ Do not referee fights among your kids. Tell them it's not your business and that they can work things out themselves

✓ Encourage all members of the family, giving attention to positives, not negatives

CHAPTER EIGHTEEN

How to Handle Sexual Curiosity

Things were too quiet upstairs where Jimmy and his twin girl-friends, all four years of age, were playing. "Something's up!" thought Beth, and crept upstairs to check on them. When she looked in Jimmy's room, she found all three in Jimmy's bed. Jimmy's pants were off and the girls and Jimmy were all giggling. Beth felt a panicky feeling come over her. She angrily ordered the trio to dress and go outside to play. She wondered if she should ever invite the twins to play again. She called the mother of the twins to relate to her what had happened. Later, she gave Jimmy a sound talking-to.

On one of the hottest days of the summer, three-year-old Gavin felt so hot that he took off his clothes before he wandered outside. When Nancy noticed her nude son riding his tricycle on the sidewalk in front of the house she ran outside, gave him a spank on his bottom, and said, "You bad boy! You can't go outside unless you're dressed!" She grabbed his arm and propelled him into the house.

Parents who are reasonably calm and cool most of the time can become fearful and upset when they find their kids engaged in any type of sexual activity, whether it's individual such as masturbation or involves other children. What causes such grave concern on the part of adults? Answers to this question lie in our own childhood experiences.

Almost every child is curious about his body and as children we adults were no exception. Two generations ago parents weren't comfortable to even begin to talk about the subject and children often learned the facts of life outside of their homes. When they did experiment or ask questions they learned very quickly that this wasn't acceptable. So sex was a forbidden subject, not to be spoken of in the family.

Things have come a long way since then, but even though younger generations have become more open and expressive in sexual activity as well as in language, many people are still uncomfortable with the subject of sex, especially when it comes to educating their children. There's still a lot of hesitation about discussing procreation with their offspring.

What makes parents so nervous? When they see their children's natural curiosity, they become scared. Parents are fearful of losing control of their kids, of teenage pregnancy, early marriage, or abortion and are afraid that their kids won't be happy. The media supports this fear by constantly broadcasting all sorts of upsetting scenarios.

Unfortunately, parental discomfort and fear in the area of sex create many of the effects that parents dread. Children are born not feeling any difference between their genitalia and their fingers. It's only when an adult shows disapproval that they begin to think that parts of their bodies are "bad" or "dirty." By the time they're five or six, if not before, kids have often become conditioned to feel shame at being naked, to be worried about touching their genitals, and to feel that the workings of their bladders and bowels are dirty. What happens overall is a shutdown of communication on the topic of sex. Secrecy and suspicion take the place of open discussion.

Childish curiosity about body parts and sex is normal and deserving of parental attention that is positive, educational, and nonjudgmental. You need to call body parts by their proper names and talk about sex and body functions in a natural and comfortable manner right from the time your baby is born. If you sidestep the subject or seem embarrassed, that discomfort is communicated to your child.

Children have always and will always indulge in sexual exploration either with others like when they're playing doctor, or alone by sexual touching. It goes on with or without your awareness. Be unimpressed when you do find out and either ignore it or talk about it in a neutral way. Yes, we're all worried that negative things will happen to our kids. Prepare them for life by teaching them to respect their bodies as the wonderful, amazing creations that they are.

Talk with your kids to prepare them for puberty, about menstruation, and other bodily changes. Discuss sexual touching, intercourse, pregnancy, and their place in loving relationships. If you feel unable to do so, there are many fine books to help you out. You can read to your child or leave a book for her to read, depending on her age. Children who aren't taught early by their parents will later turn to outside sources, such as the internet, to learn about sex. Unfortunately, they then will miss out on learning about the importance of love and intimacy.

When the subject of sex is an accepted one in the family and questions are welcomed by parents, there's an opportunity to discuss love, friendship, respect, and responsibility. Teenage problems can be brought to parents in an atmosphere of trust rather than being kept inside, causing hidden agony and deceit.

Let's examine our fears and the effect they're having on our kids. The more relaxed and accepting we can be about their natural curiosity, the more open we can be to their questions. With parental support, kids are better equipped to handle their own sexuality.

REMINDERS:

✓ Childish curiosity about body parts is normal

✓ Parents are fearful of potential problems about sexuality as their children mature

✓ Parents must teach kids about reproduction very early

✓ Open discussion of sexual topics in the home prepares kids for issues they face outside the home

✓ If kids don't learn about sex at home, they will turn to the internet or other kids

✓ Discuss sexual intimacy, respect, and love with kids in a comfortable, accepting manner. Encourage kids to come to you with questions

CHAPTER NINETEEN

How to Help Your Bed-wetting Child

"Not again!" said Ruth, as she looked at her son's rumpled, soggy bed. She and Ben had tried everything to stop Chris from wetting the bed. They had stopped him from drinking liquids after seven o'clock in the evening. They woke him to go to the bathroom before they went to bed. Ruth was at her wit's end. "For goodness sake, Chris, when are you going to be dry at night? I just don't know what to do with you!" Chris, eight, hung his head, upset and embarrassed as he watched his mom angrily strip the wet sheets off his bed and take his wet pajamas and bedding to the laundry room.

Do you have a bed-wetter in your family? I know from experience how frustrating it can be and also how much work it is to have this issue in your home. Constantly changing the bed sheets and doing laundry daily takes up valuable time and energy. You get discouraged because the cycle seems as if it will never end.

What would make a child wet the bed night after night? It could be a physical problem but certainly it becomes an emotional problem. Does he do it because he sleeps too soundly and doesn't feel the pressure of his bladder? Does he do it because he has some emotional issues in the family, like feeling left out because he thinks that a brother or sister is given more attention than he gets? Are there problems at school that need to be dealt with? Does he feel pressured by over-scheduling and not having any time just to "be"?

Please know that **no child wets the bed on purpose.** If it isn't a physical problem, it's an unconscious response to something in his life. Start thinking from your child's point of view: What's going on at school? Is he being bullied at school or at home?

Change your attitude toward your bed-wetter. Start a night time routine where you give him some of your time by reading together and talking about the day. Ask him about the best thing that happened that day and listen without interrupting. Move toward asking him what troubled him during the day. He possibly will say that his wet bed was the worst thing or mention a problem he's had at school. If he mentions wetting, tell him that you've made a decision. **You'll no longer be concerned if he wets his bed. Hand the situation over to him. Tell him that you have faith that he'll be dry sometime soon. Kiss and hug**

him and show him lots of love right then and at every oppor-tunity during the day.

When you decide to withdraw your concern about your child's bed-wetting, and hand the problem over to him, gently suggest that he manage to deal with the wet sheets on his own. Have a little training session around removing the sheets, putting them in the laundry hamper, and replacing them with clean ones. Be friendly and positive as you hand the situation over to him. If he wakes with a wet bed, changing the bed will be the natural consequence of wetting his bed and so you must not feel you are punishing him. This is a learning experience.

Tell him in a friendly tone and noncritical way that it's now his business to change his bed. Then follow through and don't mention it again. Be sure to reiterate that you have faith that he'll eventually wake up dry. Hugs and "I love yous" are essential here. You'll be surprised at how this shift in your attitude can positively affect the problem.

If your child talks about problems at school make sure that you follow up. Ask him if you can help. He may be bullied or he may have a relationship issue with his teacher. Step in on his behalf, hopefully with his approval. Gently assure him that you believe in him. **As often as possible during the day, show him that you think he's competent and that he is valued.**

Just remember that very few twenty year olds wet their beds. Give your bed-wetting child the positive attention he needs and a chance to deal with his situation himself and he'll gradually become dry at night. When he's happier in the daytime, it'll also have an impact on his night-time predicament.

REMINDERS:

- ✓ No child wets the bed on purpose
- ✓ Change your attitude toward your bed-wetter. Stop commenting on the wet bed
- ✓ Start a bedtime routine where you spend focused time reading, talking, and cuddling
- ✓ Hand the problem over to her by discussing it and offering to let her handle it
- ✓ Allow her to take over the problem if she agrees and is able
- ✓ Completely allow her to deal with her bed-wetting unless she asks for help
- ✓ Assess her home and school life to see if she's happy, or being victimized or bullied
- ✓ Give lots of positive attention during the day as well as hugs and kisses

CHAPTER TWENTY

What to Do About Swearing and Lying

John had a colorful vocabulary, especially when things went wrong in one of his projects around the house. He would let go with a stream of swear words that could even be heard outside. One day when he was eating breakfast John heard a word come out of four-year-old Adam's mouth that really shocked him. He jumped up from the table and went into the next room where he told Adam not to use the word ever again. Later Adam swore again. John lit into him and threatened punishment if he ever heard Adam say such a thing again.

A couple of things are going on in the above example. I'm sure you can spot the first one right away. John is setting an example for his son with his own swearing. His habit of letting loose with curse words is not a great model for his impressionable son. **Kids do what their parents do.**

Are you setting a good example for your kids? When you hear your child swearing for the first time, look at your own behavior. If you're someone who swears you'll hear it from your kids for sure. **The very first thing to do is to change your own ways. Choose "clean" words rather than swear words when you're upset or frustrated.**

The other lesson to be learned from John's and Adam's scenario is that **Adam is attracting John's attention with his swearing.** He'll learn quickly that if he swears his dad will come running. If John is a busy dad, perhaps overwhelmed with his own problems, Adam may not get his full attention very often. **Check your schedule. Do you spend enough time with your kids? Are you always on the phone, for example? You could be opening a door to kids' bad habits that are really ways to gain your attention.** What can you do to make more time for your children?

Quietly and calmly tell a swearing child that it isn't polite or acceptable behavior. When you hear it again, ignore it, turn away, and don't react. With a very young child, it's likely that it won't happen again. With an older child, if swearing continues, it's an open sign of disrespect. Why would she do it? Would you say that your relationship with her needs improvement?

If you're in a situation where you and your child are at odds, ignore the swearing and work on the relationship. Encourage

any positive action your child takes and do it often. She won't stop swearing because you nag her. If you yell at her, she'll rebel and keep it up. She and her friends may use swearing in a social way and there's nothing you can do about it outside your home. But if you have a home environment where swear words aren't used and aren't acceptable, and if you're on good terms with her, she'll respect the house rules.

The crash brought Liza running to the scene where her favorite vase lay in pieces on the floor. Flowers and water lay all over the place. "Okay, kids! Come here and tell me who did this! Come right now! You've been told a million times not to play ball by the front door! Somebody is going to get it!" Jeremy, four, and Trevor, six, slowly entered the room. "I didn't do it, Mommy!" said Trevor solemnly. "Me either," said Jeremy, his lip trembling.

Lying is something that starts when kids are young and continues at certain points and in different forms for most people throughout their life. It can range from outright dishonesty to little white lies. **Usually, lying is fear-based.** People lie when they're afraid of the consequences of telling the truth. **If kids lie they're likely doing it because they're afraid they'll be punished. If you've eliminated punishment from your home, you may find that lying never becomes a problem.**

People also lie when they want to get away with something and many adults do it to pay lower taxes, or to hide something they think is shameful. As kids get older, if there isn't a feeling of trust between them and their parents, they blur truths to maintain their independence and to be able to do things they know their parents wouldn't like. If they get to the point of enjoying putting one over on their parents, they have a serious lack of respect and regard which needs to be overcome. You can do this by going back to the basics of encouragement (see Chapter Three).

What example do you set for your family? You may not notice it, but anything that comes out of your mouth is registered by your kids and is mimicked by them. Have you told your partner you're not home when someone calls? Have you told a family member you liked her gift when you told your family you didn't like it? These sorts of everyday "little white lies" are observed and repeated by children. As they grow older and notice that you aren't entirely honest, they will begin to distrust you. When they reach their teen years, especially, mutual trust is essential. **If you don't want them to lie, then don't lie yourself. Make honesty a way of living.**

It's interesting what happens if you make a decision to be more honest. Lying can be a cover up for problem areas of your life. By being honest you open the door to solving those problems. Lies usually catch up with you as well. **Make a decision not to lie and set a good example for your children.**

While they're young you can teach your kids about being honest and how it's important to tell the truth, no matter what might happen. You're setting the stage for your child's manner of living not only at home, but at school, socially, and in business. If they've been brought up to be honest, and if they have a close and respectful feeling toward their parents, kids can be open about decision making, feelings, and fears.

If parents aren't judgmental, but are open and accepting of their youngster's ideas, trust develops that will allow this kind of openness. You may not want to hear what she's telling you but be glad she came to you. Listen without trying to impose your ideas on her. Show your appreciation to her for coming to you.

As relationships improve within the family, swearing and lying and other attention-getting habits go away. Stick with the changes you need to make. Be consistent and before you know it things will take a turn for the better.

REMINDERS:

✓ **If you swear or lie in front of your kids, stop. They do what you do**

✓ **Swearing could be a way your child is getting your attention**

✓ **If you hear your child swear, quietly talk about how it's unacceptable then ignore it**

✓ **Stop and think whether you're giving him enough positive attention. Are you spending enough time with him?**

✓ **Encourage all positive behavior (see Chapter Three for a review)**

✓ **Lying is often fear-based. Kids are afraid they'll be punished and don't tell the truth**

✓ **Stimulate a feeling of trust between you and your children by showing them you respect and value them**

CHAPTER TWENTY-ONE

Good Manners: How to Train Kids to Have the Basics

Good manners help us all to live together in this busy world, so it's essential that we teach our children the basics from the moment they begin to interact with parents, family members, and others.

Sydney was such a sweet baby. She loved to cuddle and snuggle with her parents, Neil and Bernice. Then one day, she yanked on a piece of Bernice's long hair, laughing when her mother responded with a yelp. She seemed to think that pulling Bernice's hair was a kind of game.

Bernice found it difficult to unwind her hair from Sydney's grip. She resorted to wearing her hair in a ponytail to keep it away from Sydney's hands and, even then, Sydney tried to reach it and grab it.

How could Bernice train Sydney to leave her hair alone? This is a common occurrence in babyhood along with cheek-grabbing and pinching. Children enjoy a reaction from their parents, but don't realize that they're hurting them. Bernice needs to take Sydney's hands and hold them firmly and gently, telling her that she is hurting Mommy. When Sydney does it again, Bernice holds her hands again, saying in a calm voice, "Mommy won't let you hurt me, Sydney." If Sydney persists, she can place Sydney in her crib or in a safe spot and turn her back. Each time that Sydney tries to pull her hair, Bernice can hold her hands or remove Sydney or herself from the situation.

What is the lesson here? The first thing Sydney learns about respect is to see her mother practicing **self-respect**. Bernice must not allow Sydney to cross the line and abuse her. **She decides what *she* will do and shows the baby that she will not tolerate being hurt.**

The key to manners lies in *respect*. When parents show respect for themselves, they teach their children an important lesson about being considerate of others. Beginning at babyhood and continuing until children reach adulthood, **parents need to model regard for others—not just other people but all other creatures who live on our planet,** such as in the case of Connor, below.

Connor, four, loved to play in the backyard. He had a special "critter catcher" that he filled with bugs and worms and filled it with grass and leaves to make a home for the creatures. Every evening, after dinner, his mom and dad helped him to take the container back into the yard and gently remove the bugs and worms. "You must let them go back to their families," said his dad. Connor happily released his captives. He was learning to have a regard for animals that would last a lifetime.

Once children are taught that they must be considerate of other people, whether the others are members of their family or people outside their home, **they need to learn the good manners that are essential for positive social interaction.** Some basic manners that must be taught are:

The Five Respectful Responses. Kids must learn to say please, thank you, you're welcome, excuse me (variations are pardon me, and I beg your pardon), and to say I'm sorry when they hurt someone's feelings or hurt someone physically. I recently read an article saying that according to a recent study, most Americans agree that rudeness is rampant in their country. Parents must consciously teach their kids these basic polite responses and become role models, using these polite phrases with family members and everyone they meet.

How to greet people. When being introduced to someone new, kids must learn to look the person in the eye, smile, and say "Hello," using the other person's name. They must be taught to stand and greet a guest entering their home.

How to be considerate of the property of others. Children must be taught that climbing on furniture, jumping on hotel beds, or running around in other people's homes, for example, is not polite or acceptable. Parents can say "Sofas are for sitting," and direct their kids to acceptable places they can play.

How to be courteous in public places such as at school, in lineups at the supermarket, or waiting a turn to use a swing in the park. Parents must model patience and regard in such situations so children can learn from them.

How to be aware of the circumstances of other people, such as standing to give their seat to someone in need such as an older person, pregnant woman, or someone with a disability. Kids need to be taught to have compassion for the less fortunate or for people different from them.

How to respect the space of others. Children need to learn not to interrupt or to barge in on their parents or others who are involved in a conversation, a telephone call, or similar situation. How can we teach them? First, we need to listen to kids when they talk to us, giving our full attention. Again, we're modeling the behavior we want to see in them. **We must ignore interruptions** telling them once and only once in a quiet voice that we will not notice them if they try to interrupt. Then we follow through, carrying on our conversation as if the children aren't there. **Instead of nagging and criticizing the kids, parents should decide what they, themselves, will do.** If we continue to ignore negative behavior, it usually stops because there is no pay-off for the child. If it persists, we can turn our backs or leave the room. Children who constantly interrupt are often demanding excessive attention which can become a form of misbehavior. They feel that negative attention like reprimands are better than no attention at all. Parents need to ask themselves if they're spending enough time with kids who do this.

It could be that a household is so busy that a child feels left out and seeks attention that he or she really needs. Also, **parents could be spending too much time on the phone or computer when in the presence of their children.**

Table manners. From an early age, kids can learn proper manners by watching their parents at the family dinner table. Training table manners can be done in a fun way by having tea parties where dolls are playfully taught the rudiments of good etiquette. This way, there's no finger pointing or criticizing at the dinner table, when out to dinner at a restaurant, or at Grandma's. Learning to manage a knife and fork might need a special session. Always maintain friendliness and try to make it enjoyable. Training must be done at home, in private, not with guests present.

When teaching children about good manners, or in any training situation, remember that you and your child are equals. (Chapter One explains this and you may want to review it.) It's important to discuss the reasons behind what they're learning and to have ongoing discussion where you encourage their progress. Avoid criticism, especially in front of others. When waiting in line, for example, you could explain that it's difficult to wait your turn, but that those ahead of you were there first.

When kids grow up learning good manners and consideration for others, they have the foundation of social competency when they're adults. They have a "leg up" in a job interview, or out to dinner with clients, for example, and become compassionate, caring community members.

REMINDERS:

- ✓ Manners training can start in babyhood. From day one, parents must model self-respect as well as respect for others
- ✓ The Five Respectful Responses are foundational good manners needed in every aspect of life and must be consciously modeled and trained
- ✓ Kids must learn compassion for those different from themselves
- ✓ Respecting the property of others and learning to be courteous are basics
- ✓ Parents need to be role models as well as teaching proper etiquette at meals
- ✓ Children who constantly interrupt their parents' conversations may need more encouragement and attention from their parents. They may misbehave to get *any* attention, even negative
- ✓ Kids who have good manners and respect for others grow up to be courteous, caring members of the community

CHAPTER TWENTY-TWO

Manage Screen Time and Screen Time Battles

Television can take over the household and interfere not only with family life in general, but with the development of your kids. With a little advance planning and some consistency you can prevent scenes like the following:

> "Mom! Sandra's got the remote! She's changing the channel! Give that to me, Sandra! Give it to me! Mom! Mom!"

Fighting over the TV among siblings is so common that we've all experienced it. You may remember being involved in fights like the one above when you yourself were younger. There are a couple of things you can do if this conflict occurs in your present family.

First, develop a schedule for watching TV. Decide how much television is to be watched during the week and on weekends and what time of day it can be turned on and turned off. Homework time, time to play outside, family meal time, and bedtime must all be considered. Have a discussion with the family to see what programs they want to see in the allotted time. Then everyone makes an agreement to stick with the schedule for a week.

At the end of a week have another discussion to see if any changes are to be made, as someone's preference might have shifted. During your family meeting, discuss what programs are off limits and which ones are allowed. If your children are young, you plan what they can view. You are guiding your kids and have the final say.

If fights occur over the TV, it can be turned off. It can be turned on again later when there are promises of no further arguments. The schedule is the determining factor, not you, the parent. But if fighting continues, simply turn the TV off for the rest of the day. No one watches it until the next day. You can say, "The TV goes off when there's fighting." Then walk away with the remote in hand.

What can you do about TV watching when you aren't there? If your set doesn't have a V-chip built in you can order one to install. It can prevent the kids from seeing inappropriate programs via the parental controls. You could also make a family rule that the TV is not to be turned on when you're not home, and have a range of other activities available such as sports, art, and games.

"Where's Andrew?" asked Don when he came home from work. Susan was in the kitchen putting dinner together for the family and watching a favorite program on the kitchen TV while she worked. Both parents had jobs outside the home and looked forward to some time with the kids over dinner. Andrew, ten, was nowhere to be found. "Oh," said Arthur, seven, "he's in his room watching TV. I saw the blue light under the door."

Put the TV in a central location where you can monitor what your kids are watching and can sit and watch with them from time to time. Never let a child have TV in his bedroom. This encourages too much television and can lead to a child having few other interests, as TV can be addictive. You can't monitor what he's watching from behind a door, so you don't know what might be influencing him.

Keep TV off at mealtimes. Conversation can be so enjoyable at family dinners (see Chapter Twelve on communicating with your kids). **If you're used to having the TV on for company while cooking or just turning it on when you come in the house, you'll need to change your ways.** You need to be a role model if you want to guide your kids to watch TV selectively.

Karen sat eighteen-month-old Sam in front of the TV set so she could make a few phone calls and get some laundry done. There were many children's programs to choose from and Sam's favorite morning program was just coming on.

Most psychologists agree that **television shouldn't be used as a babysitter.** The American Academy of Pediatrics has issued a statement that **TV is not recommended for children under two years of age.** Karen could have waited until Sam's nap to phone and she could easily have kept Sam occupied while doing laundry. Kids love to pitch in and help at any age. You can find things they can do to help while doing almost any chore. If you have a home-based business, set aside time to work when your toddler is napping. Consider getting a sitter to take him out to the park or to stay in with him for a few hours while you work.

Another point to consider is the effect that commercials have on young minds. Young children, especially, don't understand the power of advertising and the influence it can have. Parents should plan to discuss advertising, not just watching commercials with their kids, but talking about how the messages in the commercials could impact viewers.

Many of the above solutions for handling TV watching in the family can be applied to computer use as well. **Having the computer in a central location and not in your child's bedroom is important, as is developing a schedule and household rules for its use.** In setting up the computer use schedule, make sure that homework is done first and that it doesn't interfere with mealtimes or bedtime.

Time spent on the computer will vary with the age of the child and the need to use it for homework projects. The Mayo Clinic, having done much research on the subject, suggests that **no more than one or two hours a day should be spent on screen time of any kind—TV, computers, or tablets.** It should never be used as a form of reward or punishment (see Chapter Five to learn about not using rewards or punishment to train your kids).

Computer access to social media is one of today's most common parenting challenges. There are several ways you can block harmful content. One way is to get a program that can prevent adult content from being accessed. Some of the best internet filters are free and can prevent pornography from appearing on your computer. Even with these features you must still check on what your child is viewing. It's easier to do so if the computer is in a place where you can see it easily.

If your child has his own computer, some operating systems have controls that allow you to place restrictions on his user account. Again, you set limits for when he can use his computer and the amount of time he can spend. So that you aren't seen as a policeman, a kitchen timer can be set to tell him when to quit. You can also insist he uses the computer in a place where you can monitor the sites he is accessing.

When your kids are old enough to use email and social networking sites, keep an eye on it by knowing their access information and who they are emailing. **Make sure there is no personal information on their profiles. Discuss cyberbullying with them.** Make sure that they know the rules that can prevent it from affecting them. **Stress that they must not open email from someone they don't know or to let anyone but you know their passwords. Ask them to be kind and respectful to their friends and classmates and not to be involved in any**

actions that will hurt someone. Let them know that you want them to tell you when someone is being bullied online, especially if it happens to them.

Be sure all family members are present when you discuss screen time. If there are two parents in the family, **act as a united front in determining what rules are set.** If you have caregivers in your home when you're not there, make sure they know the rules and the schedule and make sure they're willing to follow through.

It takes organization and consistency to set up a framework for screen time use. Take the time and effort for the health and well-being of your kids and the family in general.

REMINDERS:

✓ **Draw up schedules for TV watching and computer use**

✓ **Keep TVs and computers in public spaces in the home, not in children's bedrooms**

✓ **Closely watch what programs your kids are watching and what sites they use on the computer**

✓ **Limit screen time to no more than two hours a day**

✓ **Be sure to stress that passwords must be kept secret and not to divulge personal information**

✓ **Parents must act as a united front and remove privileges if rules aren't followed**

CHAPTER TWENTY-THREE

Cellular Phones and Your Kids

"All my friends have cell phones! Why can't I have one?"

Cellular phones are powerful items for communication, internet use, and game-playing. Everywhere you look there is someone using one. Should your child be allowed to have a cell phone?

When you look at your own experience growing up, cell phones weren't as prevalent as they are today and only adults had them. They weren't a necessary part of your life at all. You could usually be in touch with your parents at a friend's home or at a payphone. Payphones are few and far between now, so safety has become one reason to have cellular phones. Another reason is the social aspect: kids are cool if they have them.

Not everyone can afford cell phones. If this is your situation, you just have to let your child know. And that's that. When she's old enough, she'll probably start babysitting or get a job so she can save up for one. You need to discuss her phone plan with her to make sure she has the right amount of time for calling and texting and decide how you'll help her to afford it.

If money isn't an issue, and if you've determined that there's a need for a phone either for safety or social reasons, what's the best age for a child to start having a phone? **If you think your child is responsible and mature enough to understand the rules involved in using a phone, you can start when she's in elementary school and get a phone that you can program with just a few numbers.**

As she gets older, her plan will need to expand to include enough time for texting and calling. **You need to talk with her about when she can use the phone and that it must be turned off at bedtime.** It's common knowledge that many teens frequently use their phones between midnight and 3:00 a.m., and there's a risk of loss of sleep resulting in health problems. **Many parents take the phone at bedtime and put it away. They pay for it, so they're in charge of it.**

What else do you need to consider when your child has a phone? **He must never call or text while driving.** Proper use of the phone must be discussed so that messaging is within the limits of decency. **No sexual language is allowed.** You may want to monitor phone use from time to time especially at the beginning to follow up. **Cyberbullying must be discussed. Insist that your kids come to you if they get inappropriate messages or pictures.**

The U.S. National Crime Prevention Council website on cyberbullying (http://www.ncpc.org/topics/cyberbullying/stop-cyberbullying) has an excellent article called, "Cell Phone Savvy" with a contract called "Family Contract for Responsible Cell Phone Use" that you can print out to use with your kids who are using cell phones. It covers all the basics for kids' cell phone use and has agreements for both children and parents to make and promise to keep. It also lists some important websites you can access for more information on phone use and family safety.

When you and your children have mutual respect and the family atmosphere is friendly, your regard for each other carries over into relationships outside the family. Kids will be courteous and use their phones responsibly with your supervision and your training.

REMINDERS:

- ✓ Your child could have a cellular phone if he is responsible and mature enough to use it properly
- ✓ Guidelines for use must be discussed with kids. No phone use at mealtime and bedtime are two basic rules
- ✓ Safe use of phones is crucial. Stress that phones mustn't be used while driving
- ✓ Discuss cyberbullying and ask that kids come to you if it happens to them or their friends
- ✓ Developing a contract for cell phone use is an excellent idea. See the link to the website above for information on setting one up
- ✓ If you and your children have mutual respect, they'll use their phones responsibly with your supervision and training

CHAPTER TWENTY-FOUR

How Backing Off Moves Your Child Forward

Janet is in a constant state of anxiety. She's concerned that her in-laws are spoiling her children. She worries about her husband's approach to discipline. She disagrees with the way the teacher is handling the challenges of her younger child. She often leaves her own tasks to go and settle arguments between her kids and the kids down the street.

Janet's attempts to control everyone around her will result in stress in her marriage and family relationships, as well as tension in the neighborhood and at school. She thinks her way is the only way and she doesn't hesitate to let it be known. She assumes the role of authority in almost every area of her family life without justification. What right has she to tell everyone what to do?

When someone is so concerned with how other people behave it's often because of feelings of insecurity and fear. **The bossy adult and the bullying child have a lot in common: telling others what to do makes people feel more powerful and worthy.** Unfortunately, there's negative fallout from this kind of operating method.

In this kind of environment, a child's development is negatively affected because they're living with constant criticism. Instead of encouragement for their ideas and skills, kids are restricted to rules and regulations of this powerful parent. There's bound to be marital conflict as well because the other parent is likely to disagree with some of the methods of the controller. The kids learn to play one parent against the other resulting in a tremendous lack of harmony in the family.

Children have different relationships with all kinds of people. **Each relationship belongs only to those who are in it.** If grandparents are gift-givers, kids are aware that this is the way that they show affection and don't expect it from other people. Correcting the grandparents only antagonizes them, as it really isn't anyone's business but theirs.

Parents need to discuss a unified approach to bringing up their kids and then allow each other to parent individually with confidence. If there's serious disagreement counseling may be the way to go.

In situations where kids are having conflict it's best to stay out of it. If you weren't there when the disagreement begins, you don't have the facts about how it started. If a problem happens outside the home, you can discuss the issue with your child privately later to help him solve future situations with other children. Life is full of unpleasant situations, and children have to learn how to handle them on their own.

Kids don't need to be supervised every step of the way. They're far more capable than we might think. **Every time we do something for our child that he can do himself, we aren't respecting him.** Some parents dress and bathe their kids long past the baby stage. Some write their child's essay or speech, or do his science projects for him. This tells kids that they're not capable of doing it themselves. Winning a contest with a project done by a parent is not really winning and the child knows it.

We have to find a reasonable balance between expecting too much and expecting too little. It's just as disrespectful to ask kids to do something far beyond their ability as it is to over-protect them.

Think about how you teach a baby to walk. You know when he's ready because he shows all the signs. He stands and reaches out, then walks between one chair and another. You stand with your arms out and wait for him to stretch himself. You're there to catch him if he falls and encourage him to try again. When you teach your youngster to ride a bike, you're using the same principle. You stand back and let him learn.

You can look for opportunities where kids can do things themselves while you're there in the background to help if needed. Encourage independence. Kids might be ready to ride their bikes to the store. They might be capable of making a cake or a pudding for dessert.

Mistakes are a part of learning, and we all make them and learn from them. We have to let our kids have the opportunity to stretch themselves and fail sometimes. **What is the goal of good parenting? It's to raise kids who are independent and can think for themselves.** It's difficult to let go and let our kids take over. Our instinct is to protect but **we so often overprotect.**

Self-respect is something to consider, too. We parents weren't meant to be slaves to our kids. When we stand over children while they do their homework, when we plan their Scout projects, or when we pick up dirty clothing for them, we're not helping them to become responsible. We're merely adding to our own load of responsibilities. We have rights and feelings, too. We need time to ourselves to explore our own interests. By letting go of responsibilities that aren't ours we have more time to enjoy life.

When your child says, "I can do it," whether he's two or twenty-two, give him the chance. Stand back and let him take over, and be there in case he asks for help.

Stop and think: "What am I doing for my kids that they can do for themselves?" Then talk with them and encourage them to take over the things that they can handle. Letting go involves courage on the part of parents but is crucial in children's development from babyhood to responsible adulthood.

REMINDERS:

- ✓ Parents must learn to mind their own business and not everyone else's
- ✓ It's important for parent teams to have a "united front" and agree on the basics of raising their kids, and then let go and let their partners relate to the kids in their own way
- ✓ Each relationship belongs to the people who are in it
- ✓ We often overprotect our kids. Think "What am I doing for my kids that they can do for themselves?"
- ✓ If kids try and then fail, they've learned by experience. You can give your support in the background and encourage them to try again

CHAPTER TWENTY-FIVE

The Importance of Joint Decision Making in Parenting

Who is the "head parent" in your family? Is it you? Your partner? Have you agreed to make decisions after discussion, having come to an agreement? Or do you "wing it," with one partner often becoming the dominant decision maker and the other one backing down?

Many couples discuss major life decisions before marriage, including whether to have children and how they would raise them. If they can navigate through the many obstacles that they encounter in their first two or three years of living together, they develop a strategy for exchanging views that results in a harmonious approach, maintaining and strengthening their relationship. They go on to use this approach when raising their family.

Joyce was attracted by Jack's handsome face and thick dark hair. He was strong and athletic and she soon found herself deeply in love with him. They had many interests in common and enjoyed each other's company to the fullest. After a year of dating, they set a wedding date.

When Bryce was born, Joyce and Jack were ecstatic. Bryce was an active, robust baby who didn't require much sleep. He was colicky for the first three months of his life, crying for two four-hour periods every day. It wasn't long before Joyce could see that Jack was short on patience with the baby. Jack soon left it to Joyce to diaper him, feed him, and rock him to sleep.

As Bryce grew older, Joyce was dismayed to see that Jack had a very different approach to discipline from her own. Jack could be quite strict with Bryce and Joyce became more lenient to counteract Jack's harshness. Her heart went out to the little boy as his dad levied punishments on him that she didn't think were fair. For example, if Bryce didn't take the garbage out promptly when asked, Jack would levy a punishment of grounding Bryce for a week. Once, when he didn't complete an assigned job by the deadline that Jack had set, Jack refused to drive him to his end-of-the-year soccer party. Joyce began to resent her husband as she watched his overbearing approach to parenting their son. Her permissiveness increased as Jack used his power over the child. Her many attempts to change Jack's parenting methods fell on deaf ears. Their relationship began to be filled with tension, arguments, and silence.

As the years passed, Jack's unfairness to Bryce caused Joyce to withdraw more and more from her husband. The once happy marriage was a shadow of its former self. Joyce made plans to leave Jack when Bryce went off to college.

Lack of sleep and differing opinions on child-raising started to wear on Jack's and Joyce's marriage. What could they have done to prevent their relationship from going downhill?

If you find that you're in a circumstance similar to the above, it's important to get some help from a trusted advisor or counselor.

I remember taking a marriage preparation course with my fiancé where I learned an important life lesson. At one point in the course, we were asked to raise our hands if our fathers made the morning oatmeal. I raised my hand and was surprised when my fiancé didn't do likewise. When asked whose mothers made the oatmeal, my fiancé raised his hand. It was a great example of how there could be two different perspectives on a subject, when someone might have declared that his or her way was the "right" way, assuming expertise on the subject.

Transfer this idea to parenting, which can be like navigating a heavy sea. There can be calm, happy times, and other times when problems suddenly appear such as health, school, and the myriad of different challenges that arise in a child's development from babyhood to adulthood. **When a challenge arises, a couple needs to discuss it quietly and respectfully, each giving the other time to present his or her viewpoint without interruption. The discussion must not take place in front of the children. Avoid compromise,** as the person who gives in often ends up resentful. When resentment builds up, it can cause anger that erodes the relationship. If a consensus can't be reached, an expert of some kind needs to be consulted, whether it is a book, advice on the internet, an appointment with the doctor, or asking a family member or friend. **Learning a consistent, tried and true approach to parenting, such as the one described in this book, can be very useful, as it provides a template for parents to follow, together, in most problem situations they'll encounter.**

REMINDERS:

- ✓ Neither parent should try to take the role of "expert"
- ✓ When one parent becomes dominant, the other usually becomes resentful
- ✓ There are usually at least two points of view on a subject. Parents must honor and respect their partner's viewpoint
- ✓ To solve a problem, each partner needs to listen respectfully to the other without interruption
- ✓ A joint decision must be reached, or else no decision is reached and an expert is consulted
- ✓ Learning and following a consistent parenting approach provides a template for couples to follow in working through problems and challenges together

PART THREE

Next Steps

CHAPTER TWENTY-SIX

Following Through: How to Make Positive Changes in Your Family Life

You may have come to this book with just one problem to solve, or perhaps you have a very unhappy home with kids who are acting out. There may be a feeling of failure on your part. Or perhaps you're somewhere in the middle.

I know from experience—my own and that of hundreds of other parents who've taken the actions I've suggested—that you can and will succeed in becoming a more effective parent if you make the decision to do so, and follow through with the action steps needed. If you decide to take action, and **if you're consistent and work at learning the process I've outlined, you can change your life and the lives of your children.**

Read Part One and underline it, make notes, and **resolve to begin with even one small step** that will gradually and subtly alter your relationship with your kids. Then, keep adding new ways one after the other, a little at a time, building on the foundation you're establishing as you put into practice the basic fundamentals I've outlined. If you find a challenge in one of the chapters in Part Two, go back to Part One and relearn the basics that will help you be successful.

Many people find that it's helpful to have someone there to help with the new ideas they're wrestling. They like to have a way of asking questions and getting answers from an experienced parent or parenting expert who has been in a similar predicament.

I'd like to offer my services as a parenting coach to assist you as you begin what may be the most rewarding path you've ever followed. I have parent coaching courses outlined on my website, www.howtobringupgreatkids.com. There are different options available there to suit your time and your budget, and deal with your family's concerns. You can learn from the comfort of your home, in your own time.

I have years of experience helping hundreds of parents come to terms with family issues. They handled their situations successfully using the principles of the parenting approach I've outlined in this book. Visit my site and see how investing in your parenting skills brings positive, lifelong value for your family.

You're taking one of the most exciting steps you'll take in your life. Being focused, committed, and patient, and asking questions when you're not sure, you'll stride ahead confidently on your path to raising great kids.